This book belongs to:

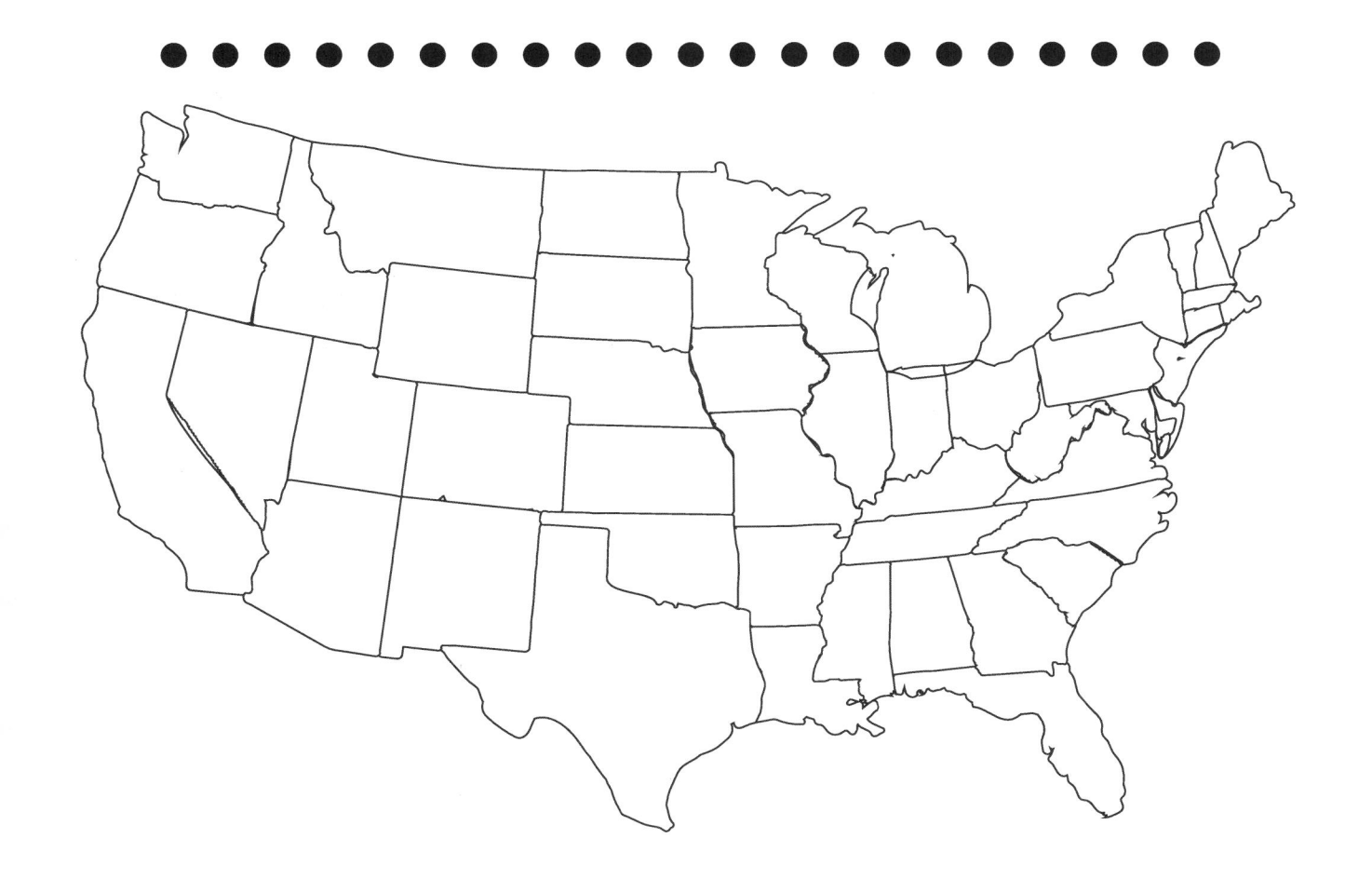

. . . .

Copyright © 2020 by Junior Press

Alabama

Facts

STATEHOOD:	1819; 22nd state
POPULATION:	4,858,979
CAPITAL:	Montgomery
BIGGEST CITY:	Birmingham
STATE MAMMAL:	black bear
STATE BIRD:	yellowhammer
STATE FLOWER:	camellia

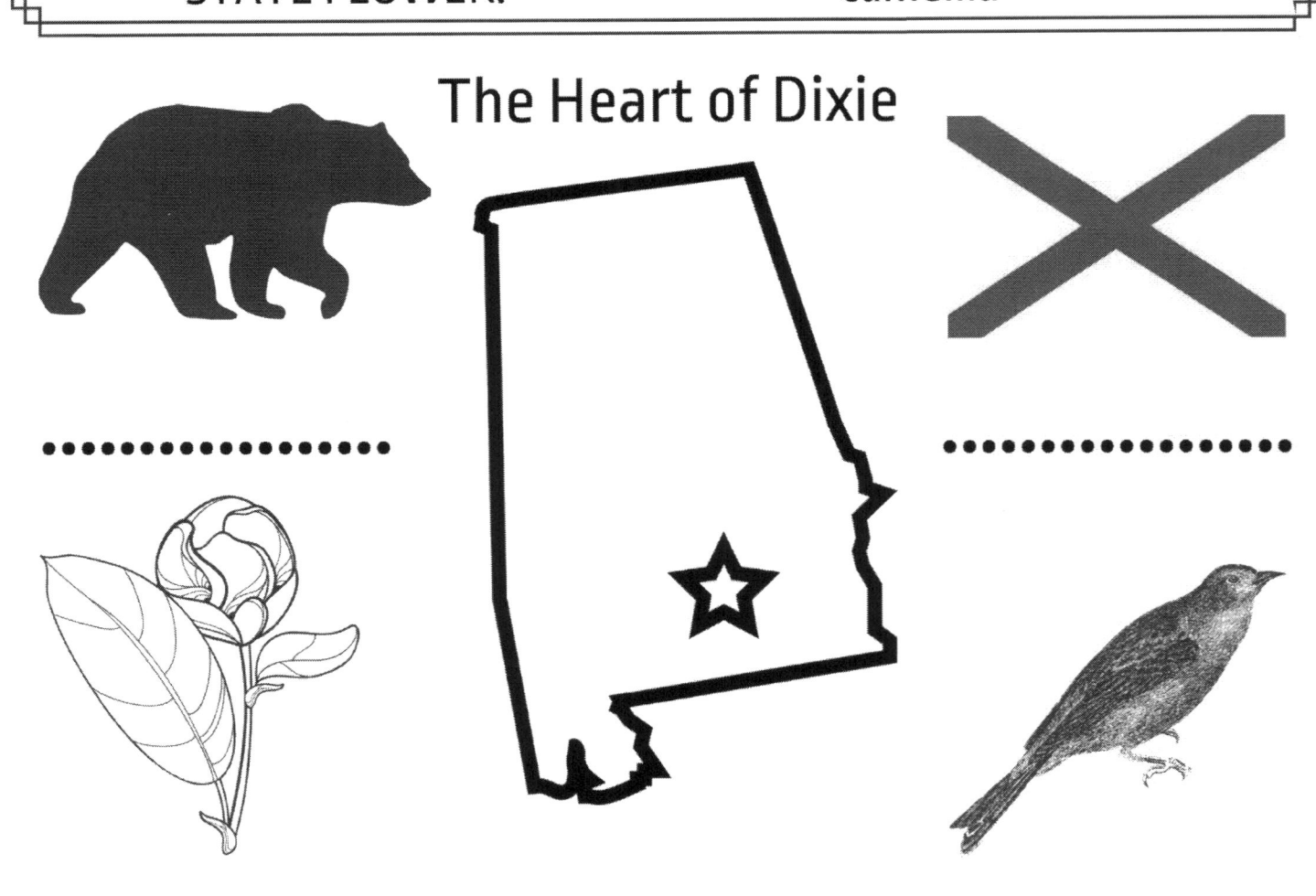

The Heart of Dixie

Word Scrambles

BAALAMA _ _ _ _ _ _ _

YRNEOTMOMG _ _ _ _ _ _ _ _ _ _

LEACALIM _ _ _ _ _ _ _ _

HAMNBGRIMI _ _ _ _ _ _ _ _ _ _

AEBR _ _ _ _

Word Match

Russell   Rim

Native   Parks

Civil   Cave

Rosa   Americans

Highland   War

1. Russell ……………… is the third longest mapped cave in Alabama.
2. ……………… Americans were forced to leave Alabama in the 1800s, today some descendants of those tribes still live in the state.
3. The birthplace of the Confederacy, the State of Alabama was central to the ……………… War.
4. Rosa ……………… was a civil rights activist who refused to surrender her seat to a white passenger on a segregated bus in Montgomery, Alabama.
5. The Highland ……………… is a geographic term for the area in Tennessee surrounding the Central Basin.

Alaska

Facts

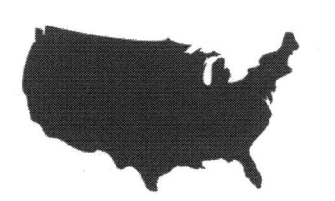

STATEHOOD: 1959; 49th state
POPULATION: 738,432
CAPITAL: Juneau
BIGGEST CITY: Anchorage
STATE MAMMAL: moose
STATE BIRD: willow ptarmigan
STATE FLOWER: forget-me-not

The Last Frontier

Word Scrambles

SKLAAA _ _ _ _ _ _

OHGANCRAE _ _ _ _ _ _ _ _ _

EOSMO _ _ _ _ _

AEUJNU _ _ _ _ _ _

WNOS _ _ _ _

Word Match

Beaufort   National Park

Pacific   Bear

Bering   Ocean

Denali   Sea

Polar   Glacier

1. The .... Sea is a marginal sea of the Arctic Ocean, located north of the Northwest Territories, the Yukon, and Alaska, and west of Canada's Arctic islands.
2. With an area of 165,250,000 square kilometers (63,800,000 square miles), the .... Ocean is the world's largest ocean.
3. .... Glacier is the largest glacier in North America.
4. Denali .... & Preserve is one of the most visited attractions in the last frontier.
5. Alaska is the only U.S. state with three bear species (.................., black, and brown), and you can see all of them in Anchorage.

Arizona

Facts

STATEHOOD:	1912; 48th state
POPULATION:	6,828,065
CAPITAL:	Phoenix
BIGGEST CITY:	Phoenix
STATE MAMMAL:	ringtail
STATE BIRD:	cactus wren
STATE FLOWER:	saguaro cactus blossom

The Grand Canyon State

Word Scrambles

OZRAINA _ _ _ _ _ _ _

IXONPEH _ _ _ _ _ _ _

ANGRTLII _ _ _ _ _ _ _ _

UCTASC _ _ _ _ _ _

NNOAYC _ _ _ _ _ _

Word Match

Juan — lions

Grand — Bautista de Anza

Colorado — Canyon

Mountain — Plateau

Red Rock — State Park

1. .... Bautista de Anza National Historic Trail travels through BLM-managed lands in Arizona and California.
2. Grand .... National Park is bigger than the entire state of Rhode Island.
3. The .... Plateau straddles the region known as The Four Corners, where the states of Arizona, Utah, Colorado, and New Mexico meet.
4. Mountain .... can be found throughout Arizona and are most common in rocky or mountainous terrain.
5. Red Rock .... is a 286 acre nature preserve and environmental education center with stunning scenery.

Arkansas

Facts

STATEHOOD:	1836; 25th state
POPULATION:	2,988,248
CAPITAL:	Little Rock
BIGGEST CITY:	Little Rock
STATE MAMMAL:	white-tailed deer
STATE BIRD:	mockingbird
STATE FLOWER:	apple blossom

The Natural State

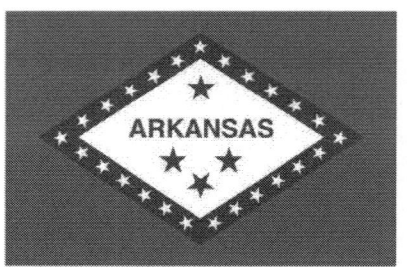

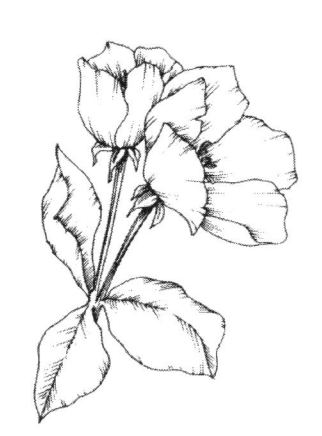

Word Scrambles

DRAZI   _ _ _ _ _

TTLELI ORCK   _ _ _ _ _ _ _ _

LPPAE OSOBSML   _ _ _ _ _ _ _ _ _ _ _

REED   _ _ _ _

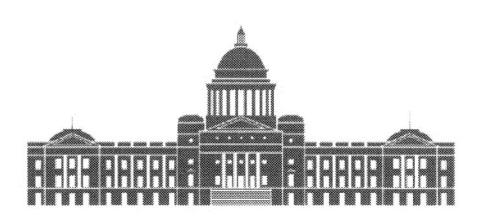

HCOITUA   _ _ _ _ _ _ _

Word Match

Plum   Mountains

Hernando   Izard

Mammoth   Spring

Ouchita   Bayou

George   de Soto

1. Plum .... culture is a Pre-Columbian Native American culture that lived in what is now east-central Arkansas from 650—1050 CE, a time known as the Late Woodland Period.
2. The first European to reach the area was Spanish explorer .... de Soto in 1541.
3. Mammoth .... is one of the world's largest springs with nine million gallons of water flowing hourly.
4. The Ouachita .... are unique in that they run east to west, rather than the north to south direction of the Appalachian and Rocky Mountains.
5. .... Izard was a senior officer of the United States Army who served as the second Governor of Arkansas Territory from 1825 to 1828.

California

Facts

STATEHOOD:	1850; 31st state
POPULATION:	39,512,818
CAPITAL:	Sacramento
BIGGEST CITY:	Los Angeles
STATE MAMMAL:	California grizzly bear
STATE BIRD:	California valley quail
STATE FLOWER:	California poppy

The Golden State

CALIFORNIA REPUBLIC

Word Scrambles

LOEGDN TESAT   _ _ _ _ _ _   _ _ _ _

SLO LENESAG   _ _ _   _ _ _ _ _ _ _

YIZRGLZ EBAR   _ _ _ _ _ _ _   _ _ _ _

ELANEGR HRENMSA _ _ _ _ _ _ _ _   _ _ _ _ _ _ _

NSAYD HSACEEB   _ _ _ _ _   _ _ _ _ _ _ _

Word Match

forty   Desert

Joshua   Valley

Mount   Whitney

Mojave   niners

Central   trees

1. When gold was struck in 1849 at Sutter's Mill in Coloma, more than 100,000 people, nicknamed "..................-niners," rushed to California to seek their fortunes.
2. The slow-growing Joshua ...., which graces much of the park's desert ecosystem, is probably the most famous resident of the Joshua Tree National Park.
3. Mount .... is the tallest mountain in the contiguous United States and the Sierra Nevada, with an elevation of 14,505 feet (4,421 m).
4. The .... Desert is an arid rain-shadow desert and the driest desert in North America.
5. The Central .... is a very large valley in the middle of California about 42,000 square miles (108,779 square kilometers) in size, it is about the size of the state of Tennessee.

Colorado

Facts

STATEHOOD: 1876; 38th state
POPULATION: 5,758,736
CAPITAL: Denver
BIGGEST CITY: Denver
STATE MAMMAL: Rocky Mountain bighorn sheep
STATE BIRD: lark bunting
STATE FLOWER: white and lavender columbine

The Centennial State

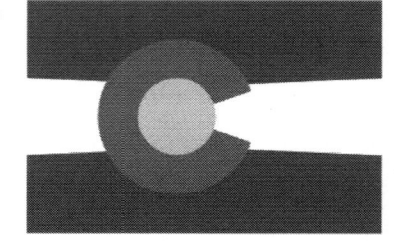

Word Scrambles

NROBHIG PSEEH   _ _ _ _ _ _ _ _ _ _ _ _

RVDENE   _ _ _ _ _ _

KRLA GNUNITB   _ _ _ _ _ _ _ _ _ _

KCORY OTNANIMU   _ _ _ _ _ _ _ _ _ _ _ _ _

UMONT RBELET   _ _ _ _ _ _ _ _ _ _ _

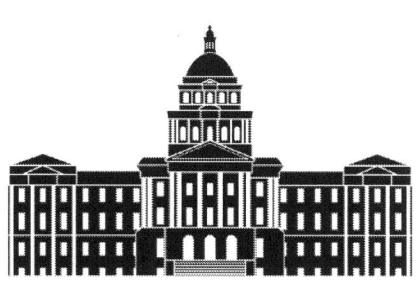

Word Match

mountain	goat
bighorn	sheep
Mile-High	Bill
Buffalo	red
colored	City

1. .... goat is a hoofed mammal endemic to North America.
2. The bighorn .... is a species of sheep native to North America. It is named for its large horns. A pair of horns might weigh up to 14 kg (30 lb).
3. Denver is nicknamed the Mile High .... because its official elevation is exactly one mile (5280 feet or 1609.3 meters) above sea level.
4. Buffalo .... was an American icon who got his name by killing buffalo to supply the Kansas Pacific Railroad.
5. Spanish explorers named the river that ran through the area Colorado, meaning "colored ...." for its muddy, red hue.

Connecticut

Facts

STATEHOOD:	1788; 5th state
POPULATION:	3,565,287
CAPITAL:	Hartford
BIGGEST CITY:	Bridgeport
STATE MAMMAL:	sperm whale
STATE BIRD:	American robin
STATE FLOWER:	mountain laurel

The Constitution State

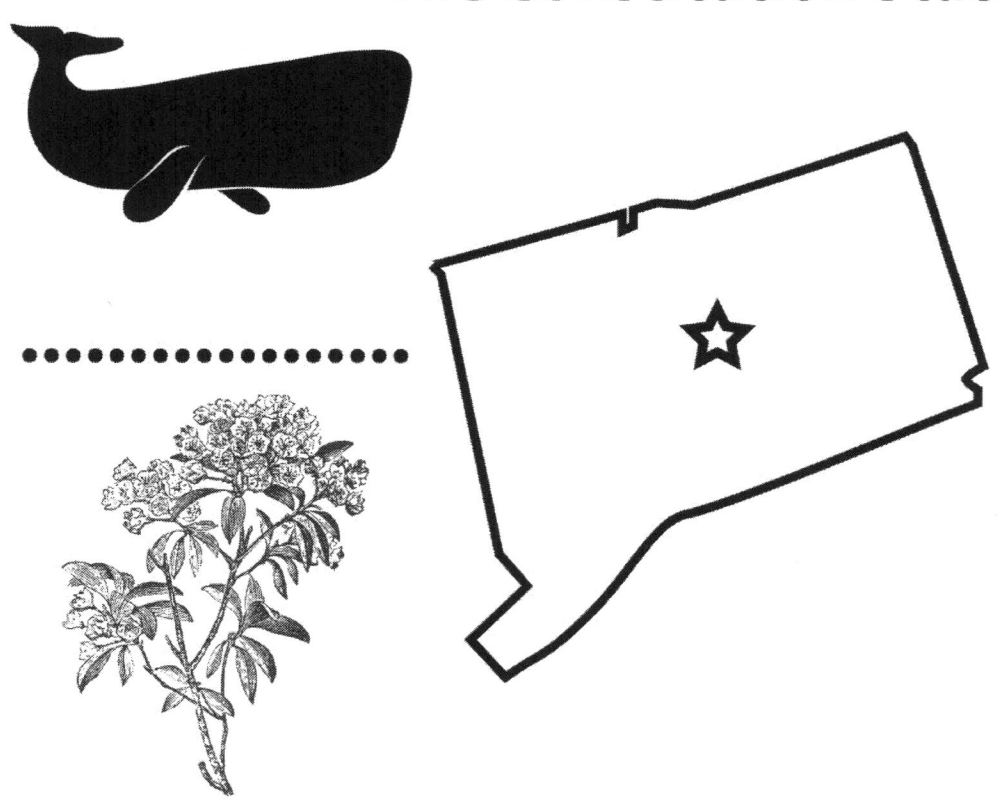

Word Scrambles

UTCNCCOEITN   _ _ _ _ _ _ _ _ _ _ _

DHFRORAT   _ _ _ _ _ _ _

IRAECANM NBORI   _ _ _ _ _ _ _ _   _ _ _ _ _

NITMOUNA UELALR   _ _ _ _ _ _ _ _   _ _ _ _ _ _

AEHWL   _ _ _ _ _

Word Match

Oliver   Lowland

American   State

the Constitution   maple

The Central   Ellswoth

red   Revolution

1. Oliver ………………. was a framer of the United States Constitution, a United States Senator from Connecticut, and the third Chief Justice of the United States.
2. In 1776 Connecticut's representatives signed the Declaration of Independence along with representatives from the other American colonies. This led to the ………………… Revolution, which lasted until 1783 when the colonies formally won freedom from British rule.
3. Connecticut was designated the Constitution ………………… by the General Assembly in 1959.
4. The plains surrounding the river, known as ………………… Lowlands, are sometimes called the Connecticut Valley Lowland.
5. The most common tree in Connecticut is the ………………… maple.

Delaware

Facts

STATEHOOD: 1787; 1st state
POPULATION: 982,895
CAPITAL: Dover
BIGGEST CITY: Wilmington
STATE ANIMAL: grey fox
STATE BIRD: blue hen
STATE FLOWER: peach blossom

The Constitution State

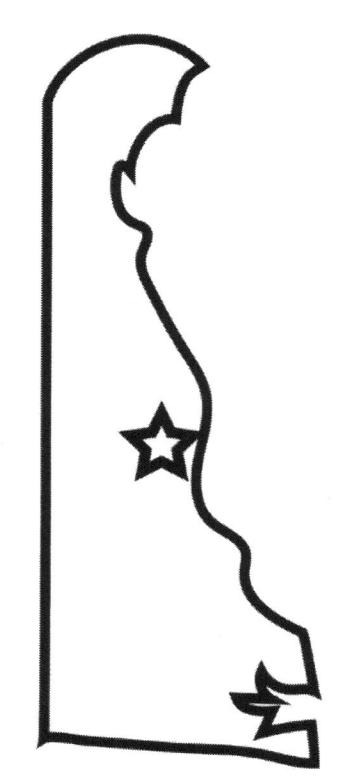

DECEMBER 7, 1787

Word Scrambles

ESLMAU RAALLG   _ _ _ _ _ _ _ _ _ _ _ _
IFTRS ESTTA   _ _ _ _ _ _ _ _ _
NAMIRACE YLLHO   _ _ _ _ _ _ _ _ _ _ _ _
YRGE XFO   _ _ _ _ _ _ _
EJO EIBND   _ _ _ _ _ _ _

Word Match

blue   River

Lord De   hen

American   La Warr

bald   holly

Delaware   eagles

1. The Delaware .... Hen is a blue strain of American gamecock.
2. In 1610 explorer Samuel Argall named the bay and river after Virginia's governor, ... La Warr—Delaware!
3. The American .... was named Delaware's official tree in 1939 when the state was the leading exporter of holly Christmas wreaths.
4. More than 100 .... eagles migrate to the Upper Delaware each winter in search of open water, fresh and abundant fish and undisturbed habitat.
5. The Delaware ....mis a major U.S. waterway that touches five different states and provides drinking water to over 13 million people.

Florida

Facts

STATEHOOD:	1845; 27th state
POPULATION:	21,477,737
CAPITAL:	Tallahassee
BIGGEST CITY:	Jacksonville
STATE MAMMAL:	panther
STATE BIRD:	mockingbird
STATE FLOWER:	orange blossom

The Sunshine State

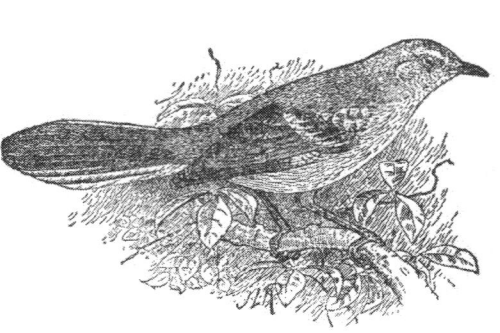

Word Scrambles

NSESELMIO   _ _ _ _ _ _ _ _ _

NHATERP   _ _ _ _ _ _ _

ORICBKGIMDN   _ _ _ _ _ _ _ _ _ _

HSFI   _ _ _ _

OSKCETR   _ _ _ _ _ _ _

Word Match

orange   State

La   Florida

Everglades   blossom

The Sunshine   World

Disney   National Park

1. The .... blossom is one of the most fragrant flowers in Florida.
2. Florida's original Spanish name is .... Florida, which means "place of flowers."
3. Traveling in Florida isn't complete without stopping at .... National Park—a swampland just outside Miami, where visitors can see alligators.
4. Florida's nickname is "The Sunshine ....," adopted officially by Florida legislature in 1970.
5. Walt .... World in Florida is known as the place "Where Dreams Come True".

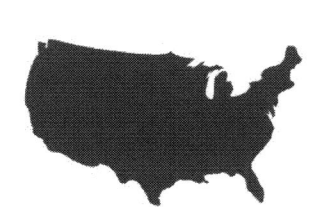

Georgia

Facts

STATEHOOD:	1788; 4th state
POPULATION:	10,214,860
CAPITAL:	Atlanta
BIGGEST CITY:	Atlanta
STATE MAMMAL:	white-tailed deer
STATE BIRD:	brown thrasher
STATE FLOWER:	Cherokee rose

The Peach State

Word Scrambles

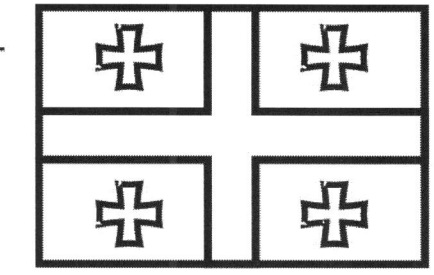

NTAAATL _ _ _ _ _ _ _

EEERKOCH _ _ _ _ _ _ _ _

AIDNSIN _ _ _ _ _ _ _

MEDTPONI _ _ _ _ _ _ _ _

TCABBO _ _ _ _ _ _

Word Match

Okefenokee — Swamp

Appalachian — oak

right — clay

kaolin — whales

live — Plateau

1. The .... Swamp is a shallow, 438,000-acre (177,000 ha), peat-filled wetland straddling the Georgia–Florida line in the United States.
2. In the northwest corner of the state is the .... Plateau, with deep caves and the 2,393-foot-tall Lookout Mountain.
3. Georgia's state marine mammal, the North Atlantic right ...., is also the most endangered large whale species on Earth.
4. Georgia grows the most peanuts in the United States, and it's also the country's largest producer of .... clay, which is often used in paper-making and beauty products.
5. Georgia designated live .... (Quercus virginiana) as the official state tree in 1937.

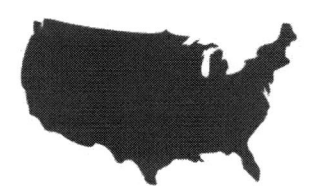

Hawaii

Facts

STATEHOOD:	1959; 50th state
POPULATION:	1,415,872
CAPITAL:	Honolulu
BIGGEST CITY:	Honolulu
STATE MAMMAL:	monk seal
STATE BIRD:	nene, the Hawaiian goose
STATE FLOWER:	yellow hibiscus

The Aloha State

Word Scrambles

LAOAH _ _ _ _ _

OGSOE _ _ _ _ _

OANICVLC _ _ _ _ _ _ _ _

AIALEKU _ _ _ _ _ _ _

UOPE _ _ _ _

Word Match

hula — Island

monk — Waialeale

Hawai'i Volcanoes — dance

Big — National Park

Mount — seal

1. The .... dance was designated the official state dance of Hawai'i in 1999.
2. The Hawaiian .... seal is the only seal native to Hawaii, and, along with the Hawaiian hoary bat, is one of only two mammals endemic to the islands.
3. Hawai'i Volcanoes .... is a fascinating world of active volcanism, biological diversity, and Hawaiian culture, past and present.
4. The Big .... is the largest and most volcanically active of all Hawaiian islands.
5. Mount .... is a shield volcano and the second highest point on the island of Kaua'i in the Hawaiian Islands.

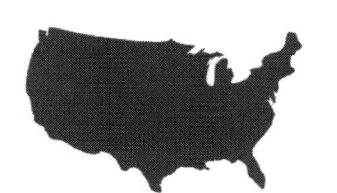

Idaho

Facts

STATEHOOD:	1890; 43rd state
POPULATION:	1,683,140
CAPITAL:	Boise
BIGGEST CITY:	Boise
STATE MAMMAL:	Appaloosa horse
STATE BIRD:	mountain bluebird
STATE FLOWER:	syringa

The Gem State

Word Scrambles

YARGNSI _ _ _ _ _ _

SLPAAOAOP _ _ _ _ _ _ _ _

EMG TTAES _ _ _ _ _ _

AHROB EKAP _ _ _ _ _ _ _ _

LSHEL YNOCNA _ _ _ _ _ _ _ _ _

Word Match

Meriwether   of the mount

gem   Mountains

Rocky   Canyon

Hells   Lewis

great horned   owls

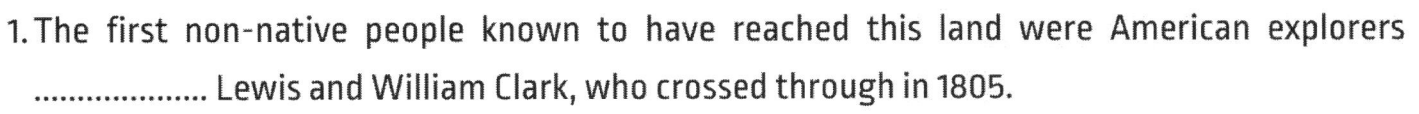

1. The first non-native people known to have reached this land were American explorers .... Lewis and William Clark, who crossed through in 1805.

2. When officials first suggested Idaho's name, some people thought it came from a Native American word meaning ".................... of the mountains." but it turns out the word "Idaho" was actually made up.

3. The Rocky .... is the second longest range in the world and the longest mountain range in North America.

4. .... Canyon is the deepest canyon in North America.

5. Great Horned .... are common owls in Idaho.

Illinois

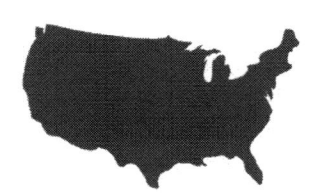

Facts

STATEHOOD:	1818; 21st state
POPULATION:	12,801,539
CAPITAL:	Springfield
BIGGEST CITY:	Chicago
STATE MAMMAL:	white-tailed deer
STATE BIRD:	northern cardinal
STATE FLOWER:	violet

The Prairie State

Word Scrambles

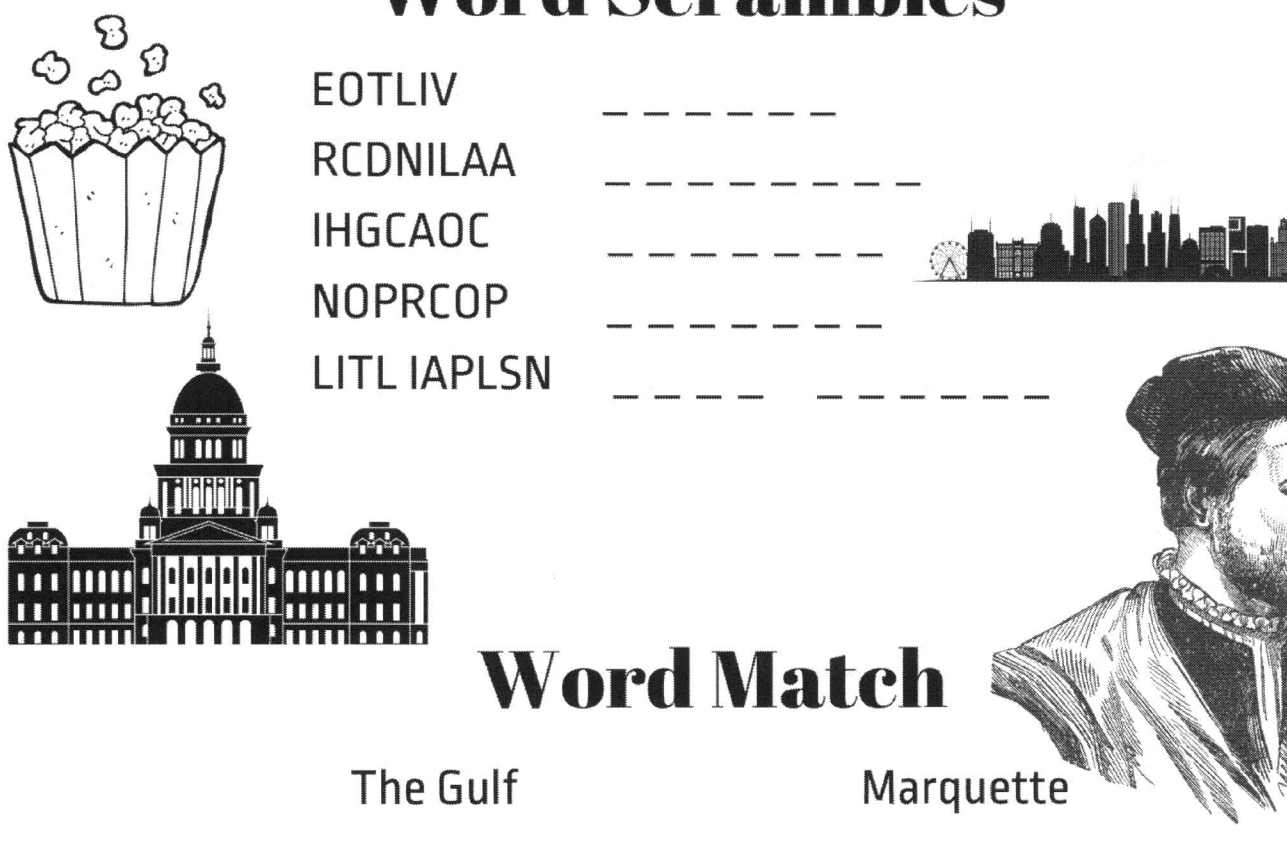

EOTLIV   _ _ _ _ _ _
RCDNILAA _ _ _ _ _ _ _ _
IHGCAOC   _ _ _ _ _ _ _
NOPRCOP   _ _ _ _ _ _ _
LITL IAPLSN _ _ _ _ _ _ _ _ _

Word Match

The Gulf   Marquette

Jacques   cardinal

northern   soil

snapping   Costal Plain

fertile   turtles

1. The Gulf .... is a hilly area at the state's southern tip. It's sometimes nicknamed Egypt because it's similar to the Egyptian Nile's fertile delta.
2. The first Europeans to reach the area were French explorers .... Marquette and Louis Jolliet, who arrived in 1673.
3. Illinois schoolchildren selected the northern .... as the bird symbol of Illinois, made official in 1929.
4. Scarlet snakes, snapping ...., and five-lined skinks are among the state's reptiles.
5. One of Illinois' best known natural resources is its .... soil. Some of Illinois' top crops are corn, soybeans, and apples.

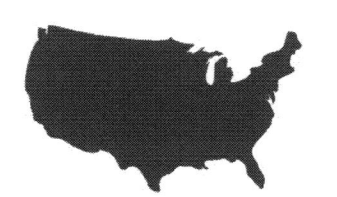

Indiana

Facts

STATEHOOD: 1816; 19th state
POPULATION: 6,732,219
CAPITAL: Indianapolis
BIGGEST CITY: Indianapolis
STATE BIRD: cardinal
STATE FLOWER: peony

The Hoosier State

Word Scrambles

EPYNO _ _ _ _ _

ACDINALR _ _ _ _ _ _ _ _

NUSED AETTS AKPR _ _ _ _ _ _ _ _ _ _ _ _ _ _

LTLI ALIPNS _ _ _ _ _ _ _ _ _ _

NCRO ETLB _ _ _ _ _ _ _ _

Word Match

American   de Chaplain

tulip   tree

The Great   River

The Ohio   Lakes Plains

Samuel   bullfrogs

1. American .... are active year round in southern Indiana, though they are generally inactive during cold weather.
2. The .... tree is the state tree of Indiana, Kentucky, and Tennessee.
3. Illinois schoolchildren selected the northern .... as the bird symbol of Illinois, made official in 1929.
4. Scarlet snakes, snapping ...., and five-lined skinks are among the state's reptiles.
5. One of Illinois' best known natural resources is its .... soil. Some of Illinois' top crops are corn, soybeans, and apples.

Iowa

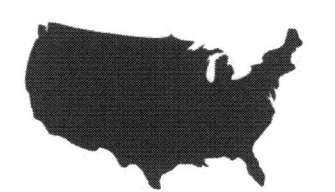

Facts

STATEHOOD: 1846; 29th state
POPULATION: 3,134,693
CAPITAL: Des Moines
BIGGEST CITY: Des Moines
STATE BIRD: eastern goldfinch
STATE FLOWER: wild rose

The Hawkeye State

Word Scrambles

KCBLA AKWH _ _ _ _ _   _ _ _ _
AKO _ _ _
ENTW _ _ _ _
AERETNS OCGFDHLNI _ _ _ _ _ _ _   _ _ _ _ _ _ _ _ _
ARUSG LMEAP _ _ _ _ _   _ _ _ _ _

Word Match

Des   Area

wild   Fox

Hawkeye   Moines

Driftless   rose

Red   State

1. Des .... is the capital and the most populous city in the U.S. state of Iowa.
2. Wild .... is the state flower of the U.S. states of Iowa and North Dakota.
3. The Hawkeye .... is a popular nickname for the state of Iowa.
4. The Driftless .... is a region in Minnesota, Wisconsin, northwestern Illinois, and northeastern Iowa of the American Midwest that was never glaciated.
5. Iowa is home to two species of foxes, gray fox and .... fox . They are efficient hunters, killing their prey with one bite that separates the vertebrate — spine — like a cat.

Kansas

Facts

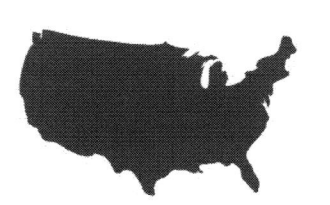

STATEHOOD:	1861; 34th state
POPULATION:	2,911,641
CAPITAL:	Topeka
BIGGEST CITY:	Wichita
STATE MAMMAL:	American buffalo
STATE BIRD:	western meadowlark
STATE FLOWER:	sunflower

The Sunflower State

Word Scrambles

AEWHKYRAJS   _ _ _ _ _ _ _ _ _ _

FUABFOL   _ _ _ _ _ _ _

WNOUFERLS   _ _ _ _ _ _ _ _ _

RGTAE LNAPIS   _ _ _ _ _ _ _ _ _ _ _

OOTOTWCOND   _ _ _ _ _ _ _ _ _ _

Word Match

Francisco Vasquez   of the South

Charles   Sunflower

People   de Coronado

Dissected   Robinson

Mount   Till Plains

1. The first European to reach the area was Spanish explorer .... de Coronado, who came in 1541 looking for cities made of gold that were rumored to exist.
2. Charles .... was Kansas' first state governor, serving from 1861 to 1863, and "an active and decisive participant" in the turbulent territorial history preceding statehood.
3. Kansas' name comes from the Kansa Native American tribe, which means "................... of the South Wind."
4. The .... Till Plains are part of a larger region known as the Central Lowland. They cover the eastern quarter of the state. During the Ice Age, glaciers covered much of this region.
5. At 4,039 feet above sea level, ... Sunflower is the highest point in Kansas.

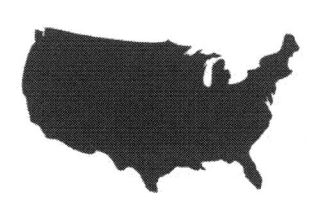

Kentucky

Facts

STATEHOOD:	1792; 15th state
POPULATION:	4,425,092
CAPITAL:	Frankfort
BIGGEST CITY:	Louisville
STATE MAMMAL:	gray squirrel
STATE BIRD:	cardinal
STATE FLOWER:	goldenrod

The Bluegrass State

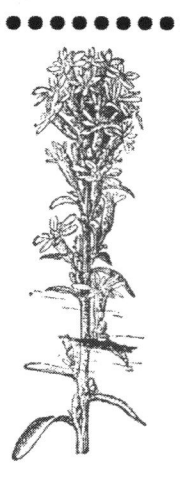

Word Scrambles

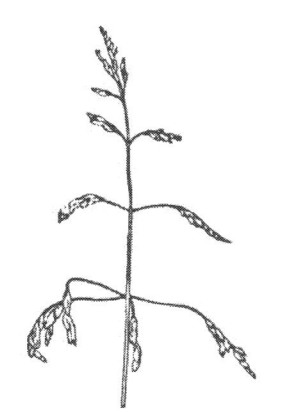

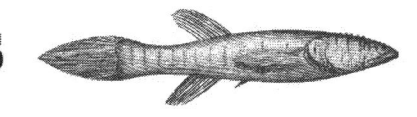

NILDB IHFS   _ _ _ _ _ _ _ _ _

UQLIRSRE   _ _ _ _ _ _ _ _

ACIARDNL   _ _ _ _ _ _ _ _

OGREDDOLN   _ _ _ _ _ _ _ _ _

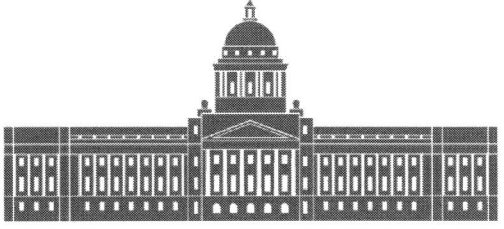

RRKTOFNFA   _ _ _ _ _ _ _ _ _

Word Match

Kentucky   bluegrass

John Jordan   Mountain

Isaac   Clay

Henry   Shelby

Big Black   Crittenden

1. Kentucky .... is a funny name, as it turns out, because it didn't come from Kentucky and lawns of Kentucky Bluegrass are green, not blue.
2. John Jordan .... was born in Woodford County in 1787. Called "one of Kentucky's great statesmen," he was governor of Kentucky.
3. Isaac .... was one of the heroes of the Battle of King's Mountain, South Carolina in the Revolutionary War. He was the first Governor of Kentucky serving 1792-1796.
4. Henry .... worked as a frontier lawyer before becoming a Kentucky senator and then speaker of the House of Representatives.
5. .... Mountain is the highest mountain peak in the Commonwealth of Kentucky.

Louisiana

Facts

STATEHOOD:	1812; 18th state
POPULATION:	4,681,666
CAPITAL:	Baton Rouge
BIGGEST CITY:	New Orleans
STATE MAMMAL:	black bear
STATE BIRD:	brown pelican
STATE FLOWER:	magnolia

The Pelican State

Word Scrambles

NPACLEI   _ _ _ _ _ _ _

IATOGLRLA   _ _ _ _ _ _ _ _ _

IMAAGLON   _ _ _ _ _ _ _ _

WNE SRENLAO   _ _ _ _ _ _ _ _ _ _

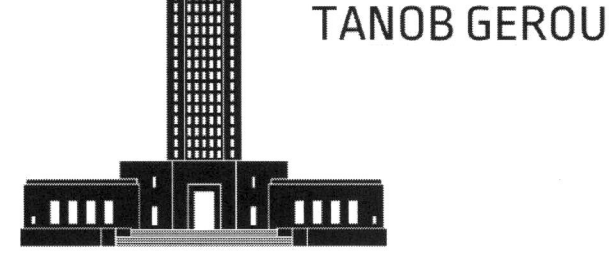

TANOB GEROU   _ _ _ _ _ _ _ _ _ _

Word Match

Hernando   State

King   de Soto

Pelican   Louis XIV

bald   C. Claiborne

William   cypress

1. In 1541 explorer Hernando .... claimed the territory for Spain.
2. Louisiana was named after .... Louis XIV when the land was claimed for France in 1862.
3. Louisiana is called the .... State because of its state bird.
4. Pecan, Louisiana hickory, magnolia, live oak and bald .... (the state tree) are among Louisiana's most common trees.
5. William ...., 1773-1817, he was a United States politician and the first non-colonial governor of Louisiana.

Maine

Facts

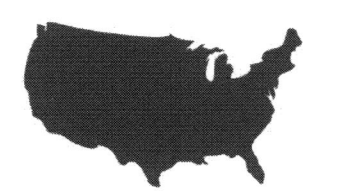

STATEHOOD:	1820; 23rd state
POPULATION:	1,331,479
CAPITAL:	Augusta
BIGGEST CITY:	Portland
STATE MAMMAL:	moose
STATE BIRD:	black-capped chickadee
STATE FLOWER:	white pinecone and tassel

The Pine Tree State

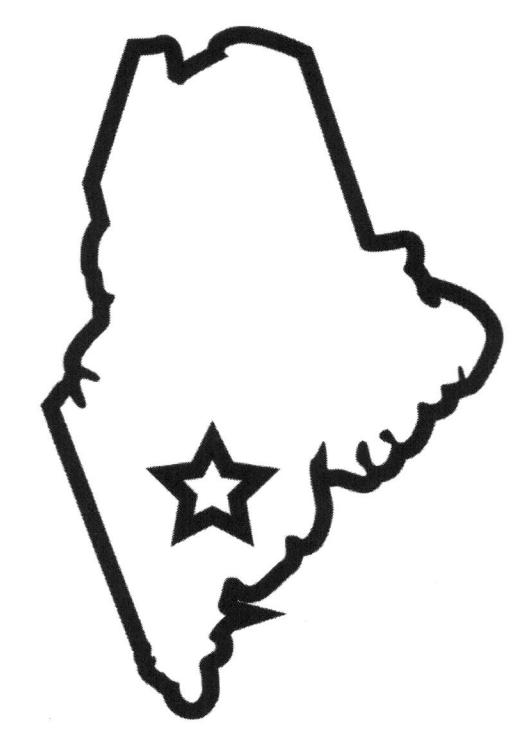

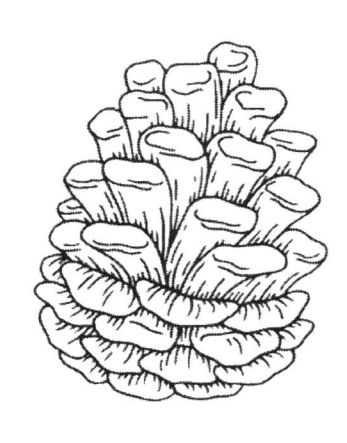

Word Scrambles

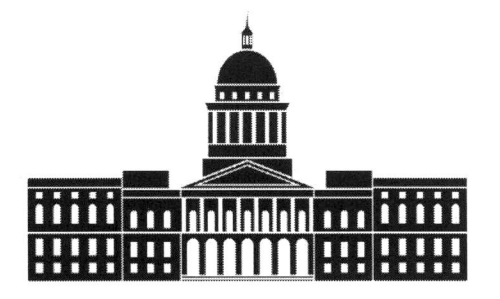

OMOES _ _ _ _ _

HSTTEILBAP _ _ _ _ _ _ _ _ _ _

CPEONNEI _ _ _ _ _ _ _ _

ALDNTPRO _ _ _ _ _ _ _ _

SASTEL _ _ _ _ _ _

Word Match

Thomas B.   ship

William Pierce   Tree State

naval   Reed

Leif   Ericsson

Pine   Frye

1. Thomas B. .... was a vigorous U.S. Republican Party leader who, as speaker of the U.S. House of Representatives, introduced significant procedural changes (the Reed Rules) that helped ensure legislative control by the majority party in Congress.

2. William Pierce ...., 1830-1911, he was an American politician from the state of Maine and United States senator.

3. United States Battleship Maine is an American .... ship that sank in Havana Harbor during the Cuban revolt against Spain.

4. Viking explorer Leif .... and his crew possibly sailed to the area in the year 1000.

5. Maine was given the nickname the .... Tree State in honor of its many white pine trees.

Maryland

Facts

STATEHOOD:	1788; 7th state
POPULATION:	6,016,447
CAPITAL:	Annapolis
BIGGEST CITY:	Baltimore
STATE CAT:	Calico Cat
STATE BIRD:	Baltimore oriole
STATE FLOWER:	black-eyed Susan

The Old Line State

Word Scrambles

AIOLCC ATC   _ _ _ _ _ _   _ _ _

NSSAU   _ _ _ _ _

UBLE ARCB   _ _ _ _   _ _ _ _

DOL ELIN TAETS   _ _ _   _ _ _   _ _ _ _

IAMLOERTB   _ _ _ _ _ _ _ _ _

Word Match

Thomas   oriole

Charles   Johnston

Baltimore   Tubman

Harriet   Henrietta Maria

Queen   Carroll

1. Thomas ...., he was the first governor of Maryland.
2. Charles ...., 1737-1832, he was Maryland planter and an advocate, first United States senator from Maryland.
3. The Baltimore .... is Maryland's official state bird.
4. Harriet .... was a deeply spiritual woman who lived her ideals and dedicated her life to freedom. She is the Underground Railroad's best known conductor and before the Civil War repeatedly risked her life to guide nearly 70 enslaved people north to new lives of freedom.
5. Maryland was named for .... Henrietta Maria, the wife of King Charles I of England.

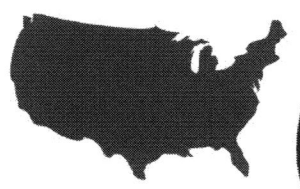

Massachusetts

Facts

STATEHOOD:	1788; 6th state
POPULATION:	6,811,779
CAPITAL:	Boston
BIGGEST CITY:	Boston
STATE MARINE MAMMAL:	right whale
STATE BIRD:	black-capped chickadee
STATE FLOWER:	mayflower

The Bay State

Word Scrambles

NTSBOO　　　　　　_ _ _ _ _ _

AREFOYLWM　　　　_ _ _ _ _ _ _ _ _

HET AYB AETST　　　_ _ _   _ _ _   _ _ _ _ _

RKRBSEESHI　　　　_ _ _ _ _ _ _ _ _ _

GNIHTKAGSNIV　　　_ _ _ _ _ _ _ _ _ _ _ _

Word Match

Harvard　　　　　　　Thanksgiving

first　　　　　　　　Hall

Faneuil　　　　　　　University

John　　　　　　　　Endicott

Robert　　　　　　　Treat Paine

1. Harvard .... is a private university in Cambridge, Massachusetts, USA and a member of the Ivy League. Harvard was started on September 8, 1636.
2. The event that Americans commonly call the ".................. Thanksgiving" was celebrated by the Pilgrims after their first feast in the New World in October 1621.
3. Faneuil .... is a marketplace and meeting hall located near the waterfront and today's Government Center, in Boston, Massachusetts.
4. .... Endecott was the longest-serving governor of the Massachusetts Bay Colony, which became the Commonwealth of Massachusetts.
5. In 1770 Robert .... stood as counsel for the prosecution in the Boston Massacre trials.

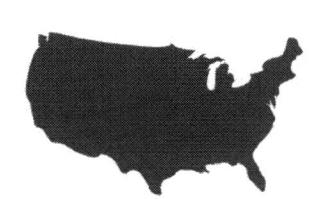

Michigan

Facts

STATEHOOD: 1837; 26th state
POPULATION: 9,928,300
CAPITAL: Lansing
BIGGEST CITY: Detroit
STATE MAMMAL: white-tailed deer
STATE BIRD: American robin
STATE FLOWER: apple blossom

The Wolverine State

Word Scrambles

TTIDEOR   _ _ _ _ _ _ _

NGSNLIA   _ _ _ _ _ _ _

OBINR   _ _ _ _ _

IGB ALEK   _ _ _   _ _ _ _

RWIVONLEE   _ _ _ _ _ _ _ _ _

Word Match

big	State
The Wolverine	Angell
motor	lake
J. B.	city
William	Hull

1. Experts aren't sure, but Michigan might have been named after Lake Michigan, which got its name from a Native American word that roughly translates to "................... lake."
2. Experts don't agree on why Michigan is called .... State ... especially since not many wolverines live there.
3. Just before 1900, automakers Ransom E. Olds and Henry Ford built some of the first cars in Detroit. The city is still called "................... City" because so many cars are made there.
4. J. B. .... is famous for the longest-serving president of the University of Michigan from 1871 to 1909.
5. .... Hull he was an American soldier, politician, and first governor of Michigan.

Minnesota

Facts

STATEHOOD:	1858; 32nd state
POPULATION:	5,519,952
CAPITAL:	St. Paul
BIGGEST CITY:	Minneapolis
STATE TREE:	Norway pine
STATE BIRD:	common loon
STATE FLOWER:	pink and white lady slipper

The North Star State

Word Scrambles

LNIMPESIAON _ _ _ _ _ _ _ _ _ _

DALY EPILRPS _ _ _ _   _ _ _ _ _ _

OIRN EOR _ _ _ _   _ _ _

ORYAWN EIPN _ _ _ _ _ _   _ _ _ _

OMOCMN NLOO _ _ _ _ _ _   _ _ _ _

Word Match

the star   Towne

fertile   soil

iron   of the north

Minnesota's   Mall

Charles   ore

1. Minnesota's official nickname comes from its French state motto, adopted in 1861: l'étoile du nord meaning, "………………… of the north."
2. Running west from the Canadian border to the edge of South Dakota is the Red River Valley, a mostly flat area with ……………… soil.
3. Minnesota's Mesabi mountain range has been a huge producer of iron ………………… .
4. Minnesota's ……………… of America is the biggest mall in the United States.
5. Charles ……………… was an American politician, United States senator and representative from Minnesota.

Mississippi

Facts

STATEHOOD:	1817; 20th state
POPULATION:	2,988,726
CAPITAL:	Jackson
BIGGEST CITY:	Jackson
STATE MAMMAL:	white-tailed deer
STATE BIRD:	mockingbird
STATE FLOWER:	magnolia

The Magnolia State

Word Scrambles

NILGOMAA _ _ _ _ _ _ _ _

NBKIMGIORCD _ _ _ _ _ _ _ _ _ _

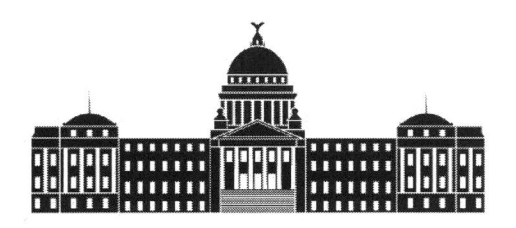

RDEE _ _ _ _

GBI VERIR _ _ _   _ _ _ _

ETH EDATL _ _ _   _ _ _ _ _

Word Match

Alonso Alvarez   State

big   De Soto

Magnolia   de Pineda

Mississippi   river

Hernando   Alluvial Plain

1. In 1519 Spanish explorer Alonso Alvarez .... became the first European to map the area.
2. Mississippi, meaning "............... river," comes from the Ojibwe language—though Ojibwe people are not from this area.
3. Mississippi's nickname is "the .... State" in honor of the magnolia trees that grow here.
4. The Delta, also called the .... Alluvial Plain, starts at the Mississippi river and extends all the way east to the state border. This flood plain has very fertile soil that's several feet deep.
5. Hernando .... was the leader of the first European expedition into the area that became Mississippi.

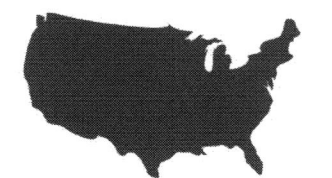

Missouri

Facts

STATEHOOD: 1821; 24th state
POPULATION: 6,093,000
CAPITAL: Jefferson City
BIGGEST CITY: Kansas City
STATE MAMMAL: missouri mule
STATE BIRD: bluebird
STATE FLOWER: white hawthorn

The Show Me State

Word Scrambles

IUBRBEDL _ _ _ _ _ _ _ _

EMUL _ _ _ _

ERAMACIN SNOIB _ _ _ _ _ _ _ _ _ _ _ _

ROHHWONT _ _ _ _ _ _ _ _

NAKSAS YCIT _ _ _ _ _ _ _ _ _ _

Word Match

Dred — Me State

the Show — Scott

The Osage — Plains

Samuel Langhorne — Clemens

Thomas Hart — Benton

1. Dred .... was a slave who sought his freedom through the American legal system.
2. The most popular legend says .... Me State was coined when a Missouri congressman said "I am from Missouri. You have got to show me."
3. The Osage .... are a tallgrass prairie ecosystem. The Osage Plains are in the states of Missouri, Kansas, Oklahoma, and north-central Texas.
4. Samuel Langhorne .... was a major American writer from Missouri, famous for his stories and novel, The Adventures of Tom Sawyer and The Adventures of Huckleberry Finn.
5. Thomas Hart .... was U.S. senator from Missouri, an architect, and member of the democratic party.

Montana

Facts

STATEHOOD:	1889; 41st state
POPULATION:	1,032,949
CAPITAL:	Helena
BIGGEST CITY:	Billings
STATE MAMMAL:	grizzly bear
STATE BIRD:	western meadowlark
STATE FLOWER:	bitterroot

The Treasure State

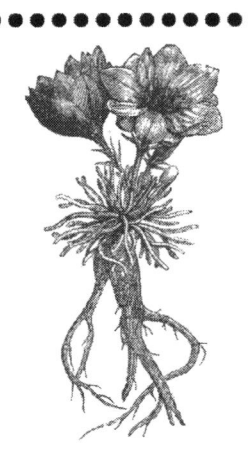

Word Scrambles

ZYLGRIZ RBAE   _ _ _ _ _ _ _ _ _ _ _

LMARKDAEOW   _ _ _ _ _ _ _ _ _ _

LGSILNIB   _ _ _ _ _ _ _

LAENEH   _ _ _ _ _ _

ATNNAMO   _ _ _ _ _ _ _

Word Match

western   National Park

Yellowstone   meadowlark

The Rocky   Peak

Granite   Mountain

ponderosa   pine

1. Western .... is Montana's state bird. It feeds mostly on bugs, seeds and berries.
2. .... National Park is in the northwest region of the United States. The park covers 3,472 square miles. Even though the official address is to the state of Wyoming, Yellowstone is actually in three states.
3. The Rocky .... stretch from New Mexico to Canada and are the most important mountain range in North America.
4. Granite .... is the highest point (12,799 feet [3,901 metres]) in the Montana state.
5. .... pine is the state tree of Montana. Ponderosa occur in the warm and dry forest.

Nebraska

Facts

STATEHOOD:	1867; 37th state
POPULATION:	1,907,116
CAPITAL:	Lincoln
BIGGEST CITY:	Omaha
STATE MAMMAL:	white-tailed deer
STATE BIRD:	western meadowlark
STATE FLOWER:	goldenrod

The Cornhusker State

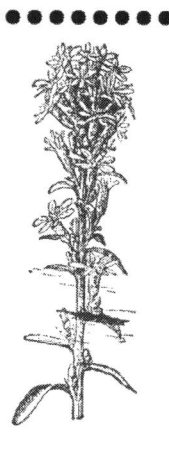

Word Scrambles

ONLCLIN _ _ _ _ _ _ _

MAHAO _ _ _ _ _

REED _ _ _ _

NGODLRODE _ _ _ _ _ _ _ _ _

UCNERHRKSO _ _ _ _ _ _ _ _ _ _

Word Match

flat — Butler

The University — Aquifer

High Plains — J. Bryan

William — of Nebraska

David — water

1. This state's name comes from Native American words that mean "flat ...."
2. .... of Nebraska Lincoln is a large four-year, public school with 25,260 students enrolled.
3. An underground water supply called the High Plains .... means Nebraska's fertile soil is perfect for growing crops.
4. .... Bryan (March 19, 1860 – July 26, 1925) was an American orator and politician from Nebraska. He emerged as a dominant force in the Democratic Party.
5. David .... was the first Governor of Nebraska, serving from 1867 until 1871.

Nevada

Facts

STATEHOOD: 1864; 36th state
POPULATION: 2,890,845
CAPITAL: Carson City
BIGGEST CITY: Las Vegas
STATE MAMMAL: desert bighorn sheep
STATE BIRD: mountain bluebird
STATE FLOWER: sagebrush

The Silver State

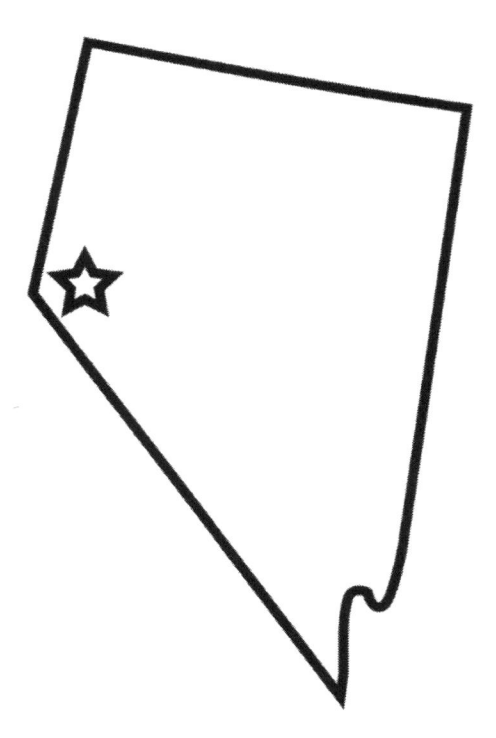

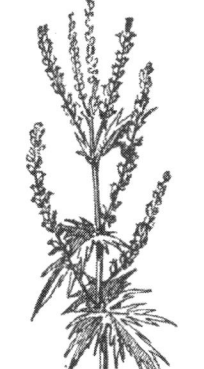

Word Scrambles

GARSHSBUE   _ _ _ _ _ _ _ _ _
IEVRSL TSTAE   _ _ _ _ _ _ _ _ _ _
OLDG INME   _ _ _ _ _ _ _ _
ASL EVGAS   _ _ _ _ _ _ _ _
ROCANS YICT   _ _ _ _ _ _ _ _ _ _

Word Match

Las   Plateau

snow   Vegas

Columbia   capped

Sierra   Nevada

Boundary   Peak

1. Las .... is the state's largest city, and it gets more than 42 million visitors a year.
2. Nevada's name comes from the Spanish word nieve, which roughly means "snow-..................."
3. The Columbia .... formed over hardened lava in Nevada's northeastern corner.
4. The steep .... Nevada mountain range crosses part of southern Nevada.
5. The region is also home to the state's highest point, ... Peak, which rises up about 13,140 feet.

New Hampshire

Facts

STATEHOOD:	1788; 9th state
POPULATION:	1,334,795
CAPITAL:	Concord
BIGGEST CITY:	Manchester
STATE MAMMAL:	white-tailed deer
STATE BIRD:	purple finch
STATE FLOWER:	purple lilac

The Granite State

Word Scrambles

DOOCRCN _ _ _ _ _ _ _
SEEMATHRNC _ _ _ _ _ _ _ _ _ _
ILCLA _ _ _ _ _
IFNCH _ _ _ _ _
ERSHMPAIH _ _ _ _ _ _ _ _ _

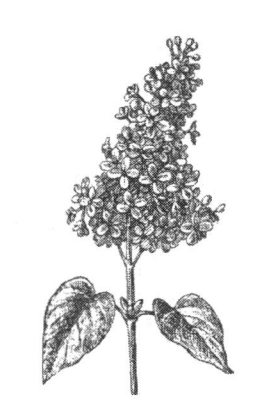

Word Match

John   Pierce

The Granite   Bartlett

White   Mason

Josiah   Mountains

Franklin   State

1. Englishman John ………………… named New Hampshire after Hampshire county in England where he'd lived as a boy.
2. New Hampshire is nicknamed ………………… State because it has a history of granite mining.
3. The forested White ………………… in the north include Mount Washington. At 6,288 feet tall, this is New England's highest point.
4. ………………… Bartlett was American physician, statesman and governor of New Hampshire from 1790-1794.
5. Franklin ………………… was the fourteenth president of the United States from New Hampshire.

New Jersey

Facts

STATEHOOD:	1787; 3rd state
POPULATION:	8,944,469
CAPITAL:	Trenton
BIGGEST CITY:	Newark
STATE MAMMAL:	horse
STATE BIRD:	eastern goldfinch
STATE FLOWER:	common violet

The Garden State

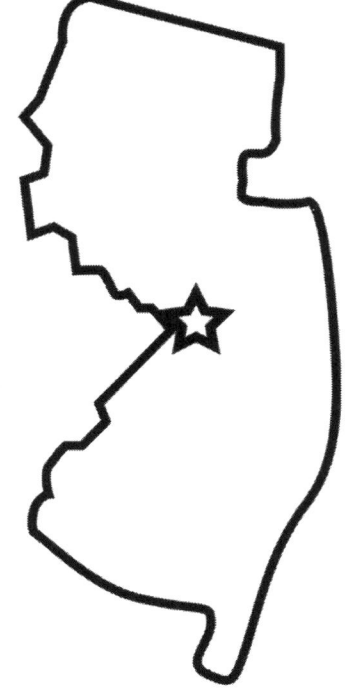

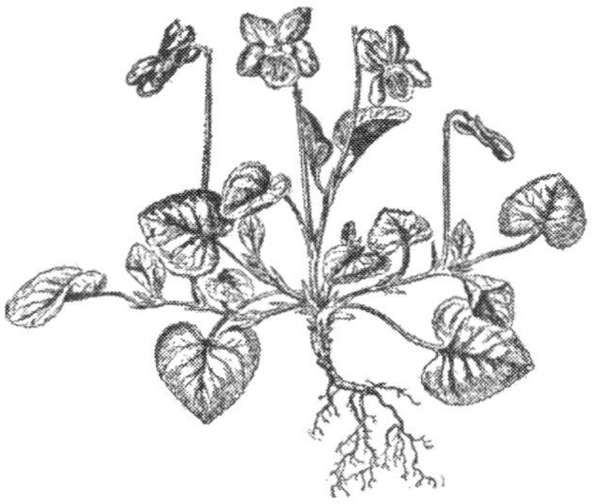

Word Scrambles

RGNEAD TSTAE _ _ _ _ _ _   _ _ _ _ _

ENRTONT _ _ _ _ _ _ _

RKEANW _ _ _ _ _ _

DCLGINOHF _ _ _ _ _ _ _ _ _

ILOVET _ _ _ _ _ _

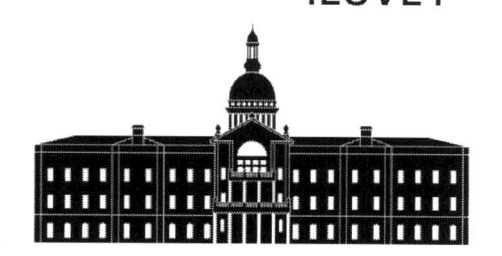

Word Match

Giovanni   Coastal Plain

Revolutionary   Carteret

George   Cleveland

The Atlantic   War

Grover   da Verrazzano

1. .... da Verrazzano became the first European to arrive in the region in 1524.
2. New Jersey was the site of more .... War battles than any other state.
3. The state was named in honor of British colonist .... Carteret, who'd previously been governor of the Isle of Jersey, a British island in the English Channel, between the United Kingdom and France.
4. The Atlantic ...., which features low hills, pine forests, and salt marshes, sweeps across the southern three-fifths of the state.
5. New Jersey's celebrities include U.S. president Grover ...., Buzz Aldrin, Frank Sinatra.

New Mexico

Facts

STATEHOOD: 1912; 47th state
POPULATION: 2,085,109
CAPITAL: Santa Fe
BIGGEST CITY: Albuquerque
STATE MAMMAL: black bear
STATE BIRD: greater roadrunner
STATE FLOWER: yucca

Land of Enchantment

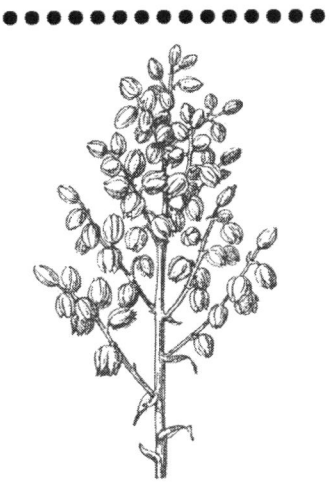

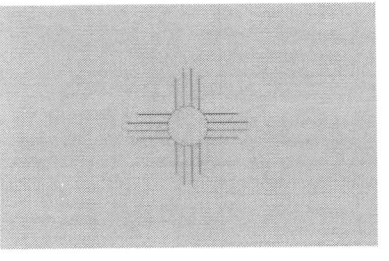

Word Scrambles

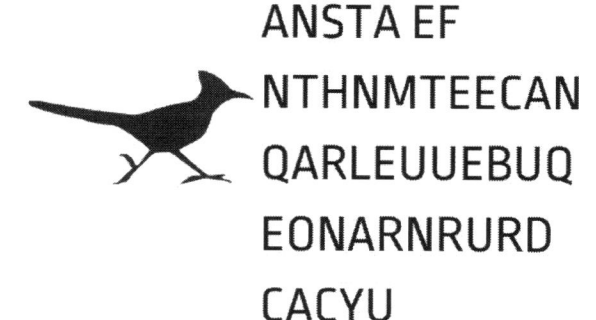

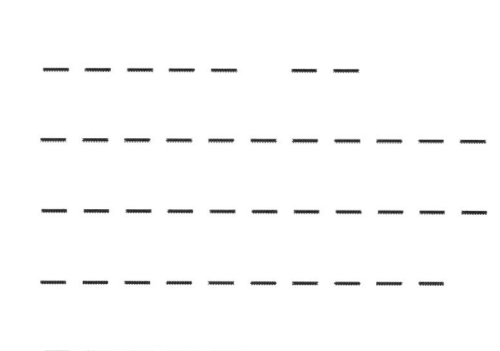

ANSTA EF _ _ _ _ _   _ _

NTHNMTEECAN _ _ _ _ _ _ _ _ _ _ _

QARLEUUEBUQ _ _ _ _ _ _ _ _ _ _ _

EONARNRURD _ _ _ _ _ _ _ _ _ _

CACYU _ _ _ _ _

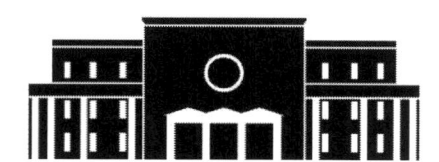

Word Match

Bering   Mexico

Francisco Vázquez   Strait

Nueva   de Coronado

Land   of Enchantment

Carlsbad   Caverns

1. People came to the area that's now New Mexico more than 12,000 years ago. Experts think they migrated from what's now Russia across a land bridge called the .... Strait.
2. In 1540 Spanish explorer Francisco Vázquez .... came to the area in search of cities made of gold that were rumored to exist in the Americas.
3. When the Spanish set out to explore the region, they hoped to find land as valuable as what they'd found earlier in Mexico. So they dubbed the area .... Mexico.
4. The nickname for New Mexico is "The Land ...." because of its beauty.
5. The area also features .... Caverns, which has more than 119 caves to explore.

New York

Facts

STATEHOOD:　　　　　　　　1788; 11th state
POPULATION:　　　　　　　　19,795,791
CAPITAL:　　　　　　　　　　Albany
BIGGEST CITY:　　　　　　　New York
STATE MAMMAL:　　　　　　beaver
STATE BIRD:　　　　　　　　bluebird
STATE FLOWER:　　　　　　rose

The Empire State

Word Scrambles

RPEEMI ESTTA _ _ _ _ _ _   _ _ _ _ _

BNALAY _ _ _ _ _

EWN OKRY _ _ _   _ _ _ _

UBRDBLIE _ _ _ _ _ _ _ _

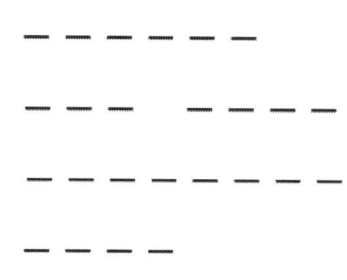

SOER _ _ _ _

Word Match

New   Washington

George   maple

the British   Amsterdam

sugar   Duke of York

Mount   Marcy

1. In 1624 the Dutch established a colony on what's now Manhattan Island called New .... It was renamed New York once the British took control of the area in 1664.
2. George .... was sworn in as the United States' first president in New York City.
3. New York was named after the British .... Many experts believe it's nicknamed the Empire State because George Washington called New York "the seat of the Empire".
4. The sugar .... was adopted as New York State tree in 1956 in recognition of it value.
5. The Adirondack Upland, known for the Appalachian Mountains and its forests, waterfalls, and lakes includes New York's highest peak, ... Marcy.

North Carolina

Facts

STATEHOOD:	1789; 12th state
POPULATION:	10,488,084
CAPITAL:	Raleigh
BIGGEST CITY:	Charlotte
STATE MAMMAL:	gray squirrel
STATE BIRD:	cardinal
STATE FLOWER:	flowering dogwood

The Tar Heel State

Word Scrambles

AERIHGL   _ _ _ _ _ _ _

OTRTHELAC   _ _ _ _ _ _ _ _ _

LCNADIAR   _ _ _ _ _ _ _ _

OGOWDDO   _ _ _ _ _ _ _

ART LHEE   _ _ _   _ _ _ _

Word Match

the Tar   Howe

coastal   Blackbeard

The pirate   plain

Robert   Hewes

Joseph   Heel State

1. North Carolina got the nickname .... Heel State because workers here used to sell tar, pitch, and turpentine from the state's longleaf pine trees to be used in wooden ships.
2. The eastern region is called the .... plain
3. The pirate .... called North Carolina home, and spent time ransacking ships off the coast in the early 1700s.
4. .... Howe, 1732-1786, he was a continental army general from North Carolina during the American revolutionary war.
5. Joseph .... was signer of the Declaration of Independence representing North Carolina.

North Dakota

Facts

STATEHOOD:	1889; 39th state
POPULATION:	756,927
CAPITAL:	Bismarck
BIGGEST CITY:	Fargo
STATE TREE:	American elm
STATE BIRD:	western meadowlark
STATE FLOWER:	wild prairie rose

The Peace Garden State

Word Scrambles

IANMCARE MEL _ _ _ _ _ _ _ _ _ _ _

OKADRLEMAW _ _ _ _ _ _ _ _ _ _

RIRIAPE ERSO _ _ _ _ _ _ _ _ _ _

GARFO _ _ _ _ _

MABSKRCI _ _ _ _ _ _ _ _

Word Match

Pierre Gault   Plateau

Native American   La Vérendrye

Missouri   coal

American   Sioux

brown   elm

1. France controlled the area after an explorer named .... La Vérendrye became the first European to arrive, in 1738.
2. Dakota is a Native American .... word that roughly means "friend" or "ally."
3. West of the Drift Prairie is the .... Plateau, the state's highest region.
4. The American .... became North Dakota's state tree in 1947. A common tree across the state, it often reaches a height of 120 feet or more.
5. North Dakota contains the world's biggest deposit of lignite, a type of soft, ... coal.

Ohio

Facts

STATEHOOD:	1803; 17th state
POPULATION:	11,614,373
CAPITAL:	Columbus
BIGGEST CITY:	Columbus
STATE MAMMAL:	White-tailed deer
STATE BIRD:	cardinal
STATE FLOWER:	red carnation

The Buckeye State

Word Scrambles

YUKCEBE TTSEA _ _ _ _ _ _ _ _ _ _ _

LCMOBSUU _ _ _ _ _ _ _ _

NACROITNA _ _ _ _ _ _ _ _

NIARALDC _ _ _ _ _ _ _

RDEE _ _ _ _

Word Match

Robert — Tiffin

Lake Erie — de La Salle

The Buckeye — Harris

Edward — State

William Henry — Canal

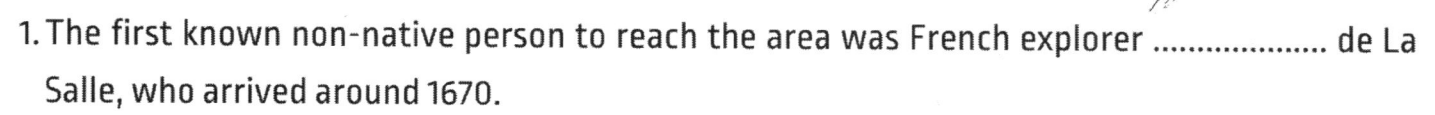

1. The first known non-native person to reach the area was French explorer .... de La Salle, who arrived around 1670.
2. Ohio became the 17th state in 1803. The Ohio and .... Canal opened almost 30 years later and connected Lake Erie with the Ohio River.
3. The Buckeye .... gets its nickname from a common tree in Ohio called a buckeye.
4. Edward ...., 1766-1829, he was a politician and first governor of Ohio.
5. William Henry ...., 1773-1841, he was an American military officer, United States senator from Ohio, and the ninth president of the United States.

Oklahoma

Facts

STATEHOOD:	1907; 46th state
POPULATION:	3,923,561
CAPITAL:	Oklahoma City
BIGGEST CITY:	Oklahoma City
STATE MAMMAL:	buffalo
STATE BIRD:	scissor-tailed flycatcher
STATE FLOWER:	Oklahoma rose

The Sooner State

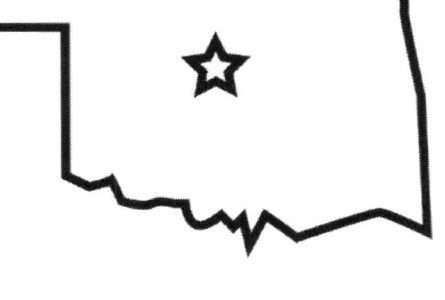

Word Scrambles

ECRHYTLFAC _ _ _ _ _ _ _ _ _ _

LOMAOHAK YCTI _ _ _ _ _ _ _ _ _ _ _ _

NSROOE TATES _ _ _ _ _ _ _ _ _ _

LFBAUOF _ _ _ _ _ _ _

DDBREU _ _ _ _ _ _

Word Match

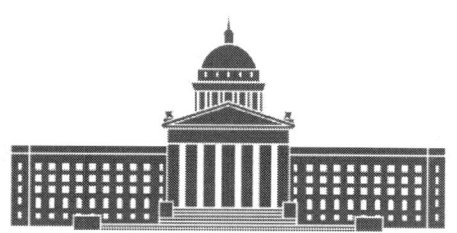

Francisco Vásquez   de Coronado

Choctaw   State

the Sooner   language

The High   Plains

Captain   W. L. Couch

1. Spanish explorer Francisco Vásquez .... traveled to the region in 1541 searching for fabled cities made of gold.
2. The word Oklahoma is a combination of two words in the .... language, which is spoken by the Choctaw people.
3. The U.S. state of Oklahoma has been popularly nicknamed the "Sooner ....".
4. The High .... are flat grasslands in the northwest.
5. .... W. L. Couch was famous as a leader of the Boomer Movement and as the first provisional mayor of Oklahoma City.

Oregon

Facts

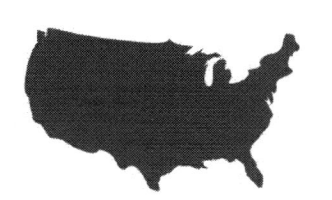

STATEHOOD:	1859; 33rd state
POPULATION:	4,093,465
CAPITAL:	Salem
BIGGEST CITY:	Portland
STATE MAMMAL:	American beaver
STATE BIRD:	western meadowlark
STATE FLOWER:	Oregon grape

The Beaver State

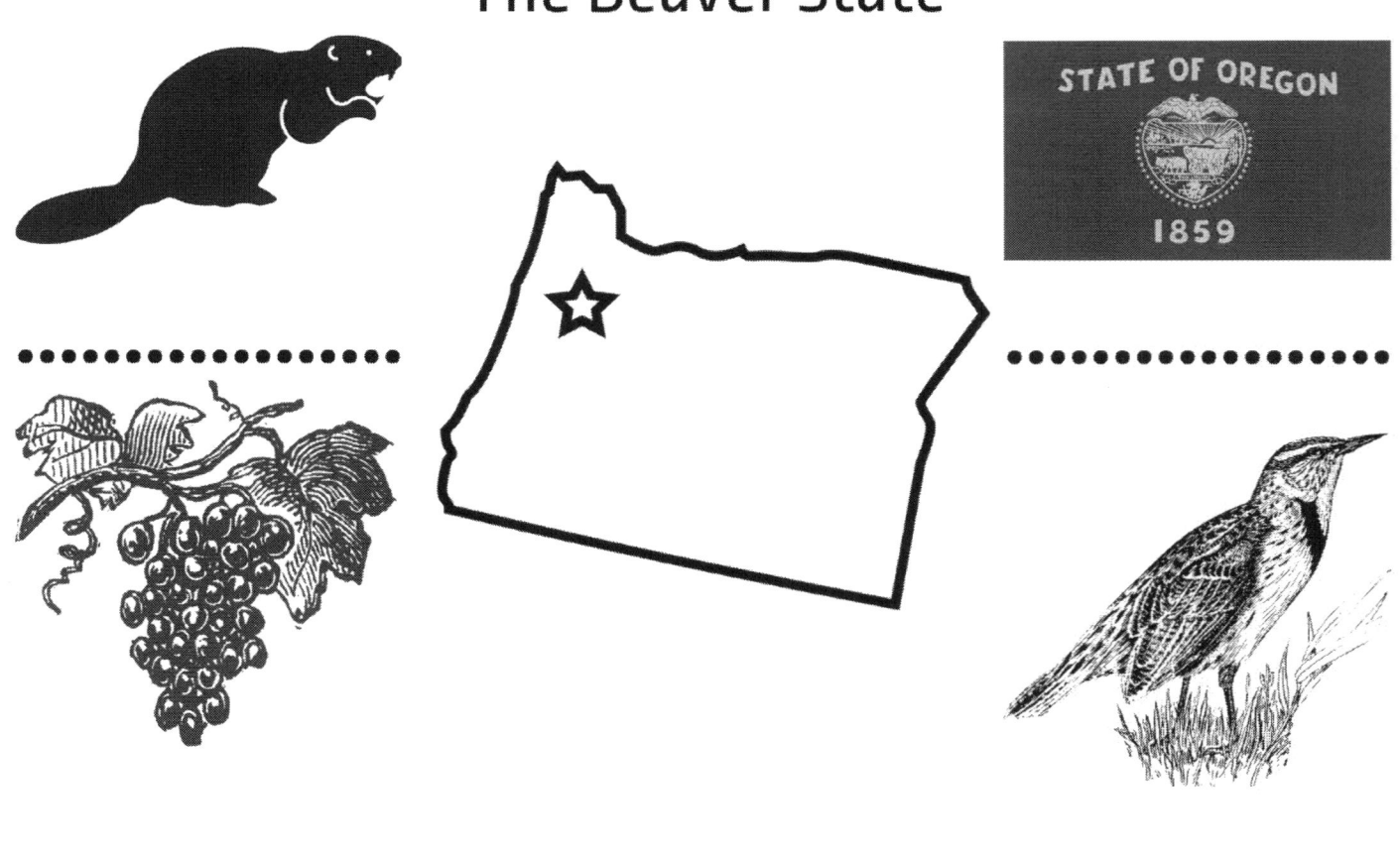

Word Scrambles

ESALM _ _ _ _ _

NROTLPDA _ _ _ _ _ _ _ _

PAGER _ _ _ _ _

VEBEAR _ _ _ _ _ _

LORDKWMEAA _ _ _ _ _ _ _ _ _ _

Word Match

Thomas   Oregon

Beaver   Hood

oregon   State

Mount   grape

USS   Jefferson

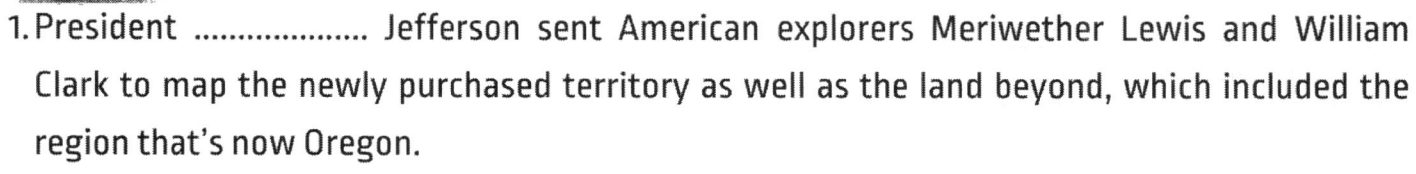

1. President .... Jefferson sent American explorers Meriwether Lewis and William Clark to map the newly purchased territory as well as the land beyond, which included the region that's now Oregon.

2. Oregon was nicknamed the Beaver .... because early settlers used to trap these animals for their fur.

3. Oregon .... became the Oregon State Flower on July 18, 1892.

4. Oregon's highest point is Mount .... (11,245 feet).

5. .... Oregon was a pre Dreadnought Indiana class battleship of the United States Navy.

Pennsylvania

Facts

STATEHOOD:	1787; 2nd state
POPULATION:	12,784,227
CAPITAL:	Harrisburg
BIGGEST CITY:	Philadelphia
STATE MAMMAL:	white-tailed deer
STATE BIRD:	ruffed grouse
STATE FLOWER:	mountain laurel

The Keystone State

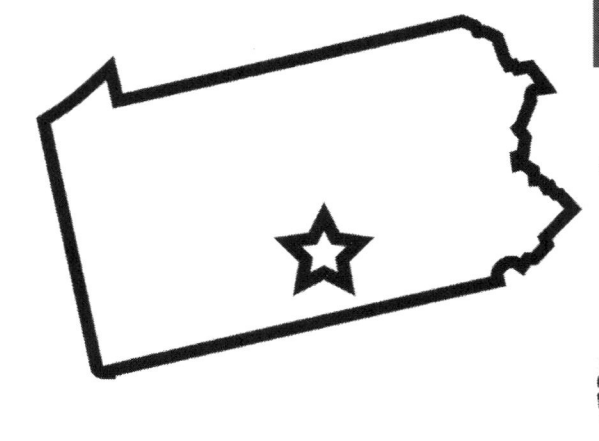

Word Scrambles

EOYKNSET TTSAE _ _ _ _ _ _ _   _ _ _ _ _

GBRRUHAIRS _ _ _ _ _ _ _ _ _ _

ILALDAHPHPIE _ _ _ _ _ _ _ _ _ _ _ _

ERULLA _ _ _ _ _ _

EOUGSR _ _ _ _ _ _

Word Match

William   Bell

Penns   woods

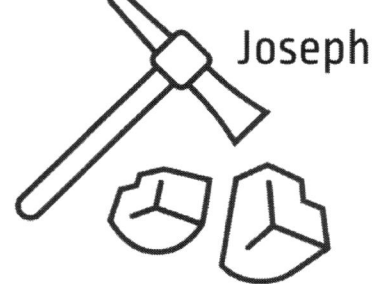

coal   mining

Liberty   Penn

Joseph   Reed

1. The name "Pennsylvania" was created by William .... to honor his father.
2. Pennsylvania is a combination of Latin words that together mean "Penn's ...."
3. Pennsylvania is one of the top states for .... mining.
4. The Liberty .... is an iconic symbol of American independence, located in Philadelphia, Pennsylvania.
5. Joseph ...., 1741-1785, he was a lawyer, military officer and statesman from Pennsylvania.

Rhode Island

Facts

STATEHOOD:	1790; 13th state
POPULATION:	1,056,426
CAPITAL:	Providence
BIGGEST CITY:	Providence
MARINE MAMMAL:	Harbor seal
STATE BIRD:	Rhode Island red chicken
STATE FLOWER:	violet

The Ocean State

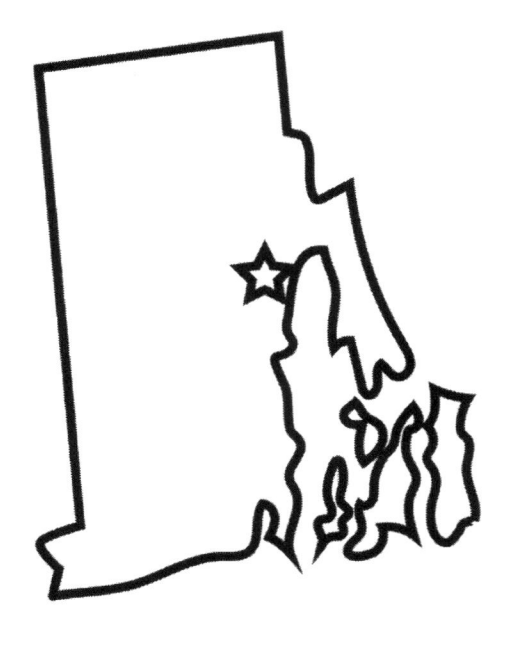

Word Scrambles

LVTIOE _ _ _ _ _ _

OEINDEVPCR _ _ _ _ _ _ _ _ _ _

CANOE TTSEA _ _ _ _ _ _ _ _ _

EDR KINECHC _ _ _ _ _ _ _ _ _

LINDAS _ _ _ _ _ _

Word Match

Giovanni   da Verrazzano

Adriaen   Williams

Jerimoth   Burnside

Roger   Hill

General   Block

1. Italian explorer .... da Verrazzano explored the area in 1524.
2. Dutch explorer Adriaen .... called the land Roodt Eylandt, meaning "red island," because of the red clay at its shore—and the name later evolved into Rhode Island.
3. Rhode Island's highest point is Jerimoth ....
4. Roger ...., 1603-1683, he was an English theologian and co-founder of Rhode Island.
5. General .... (1824–1881) was an American soldier, railroad executive, inventor, industrialist, and politician from Rhode Island. He served as the Governor of Rhode Island from 1866 to 1869, and as a United States Senator for Rhode Island from 1875 until his death.

South Carolina

Facts

STATEHOOD:	1788; 8th state
POPULATION:	4,961,119
CAPITAL:	Columbia
BIGGEST CITY:	Columbia
STATE MAMMAL:	white-tailed deer
STATE BIRD:	Carolina wren
STATE FLOWER:	yellow jessamine

The Palmetto State

Word Scrambles

MOLCUAIB   _ _ _ _ _ _ _ _

INRALCOA   _ _ _ _ _ _ _ _

NWER   _ _ _ _

ENIEJSMSA   _ _ _ _ _ _ _ _ _

LOTTMAEP TSTEA   _ _ _ _ _ _ _   _ _ _ _ _

Word Match

King   palmetto

Palmetto   Charles I

cabbage   Mountain

Sassafras   Wilkinson Pickens

Francis   State

1. The Carolinas were named after .... Charles I of England.
2. The state's nickname, the .... State, was coined in honor of the state tree, the sabal palmetto.
3. Cabbage .... is the state tree of South Carolina and Florida.
4. The Blue Ridge Mountain Province stretches across northwestern South Carolina. Its forested peaks include the state's highest point, ... Mountain.
5. .... Wilkinson Pickens, he was a political democrat and governor of South Carolina.

South Dakota

Facts

STATEHOOD: 1889; 40th state
POPULATION: 858,469
CAPITAL: Pierre
BIGGEST CITY: Sioux Falls
STATE MAMMAL: coyote
STATE BIRD: Ring-necked pheasant
STATE FLOWER: Pasque flower

The Mount Rushmore State

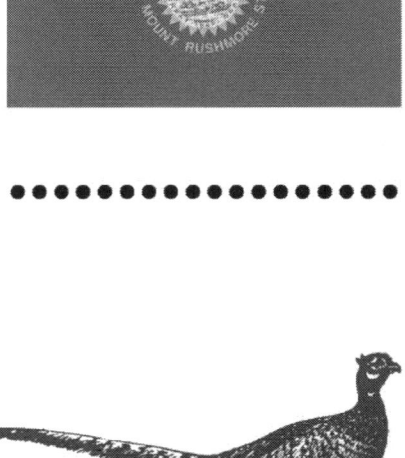

Word Scrambles

EIPRER _ _ _ _ _ _

UXSIO SLLFA _ _ _ _ _ _ _ _ _ _

EAQUSP _ _ _ _ _ _

ATEHPNAS _ _ _ _ _ _ _ _

YTCEOO _ _ _ _ _ _

Word Match

South   Peak

Vérendrye   Rushmore

Native American brothers

Mount   Sioux

Black Elk   Dakota

1. South ………………… winters are dry with snowfall averages that range from 31 inches in the much warmer eastern part of the state to 198 inches in the deadly cold western part of the state.
2. The first Europeans in the area were the Vérendrye ………………., who claimed it for France in 1743.
3. Dakota is a Native American ………………… word that means roughly "friendly" or "allies."
4. The state's nickname comes from ………………… Rushmore, an enormous sculpture.
5. The Black Hills in the southwest is a range of mountains that includes the 7,242-foot Black Elk ………………., the state's highest point.

Tennessee

Facts

STATEHOOD: 1796; 16th state
POPULATION: 6,651,194
CAPITAL: Nashville
BIGGEST CITY: Memphis
STATE MAMMAL: raccoon
STATE BIRD: mockingbird
STATE FLOWER: iris

The Volunteer State

Word Scrambles

LLNHISVAE　　＿＿＿＿＿＿＿＿＿

IMESMPH　　　＿＿＿＿＿＿＿

KBIONDCRIGM　＿＿＿＿＿＿＿＿＿＿

SRII　　　　　＿＿＿＿

RTOELUENV　　＿＿＿＿＿＿＿＿

Word Match

Hernando　　　　　　　de Soto

Tanasi and　　　　　　Mountain

Mexican-　　　　　　　American War

Lookout　　　　　　　 Knox Polk

James　　　　　　　　 Tanasqui

1. Spanish explorer .... de Soto was the first known European to reach the land now called Tennessee, in 1540.
2. No one's sure how Tennessee got its name, but two Native American villages were called Tanasi and ...., which sound similar to "Tennessee."
3. During the War of 1812, an estimated 20,000 troops volunteered to fight, and in 1846, 30,000 Tennesseans enlisted for the ....American War.
4. Lookout .... has views of seven states.
5. .... Knox Polk, 1795-1849, he was the eleventh president of the United States, speaker of the house of representatives and governor of Tennessee.

Texas

Facts

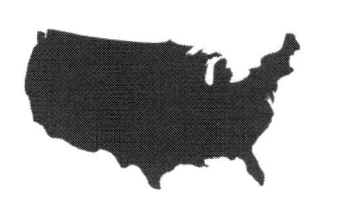

STATEHOOD:	1845; 28th state
POPULATION:	27,469,114
CAPITAL:	Austin
BIGGEST CITY:	Houston
STATE LARGE ANIMAL:	Texas longhorn
STATE BIRD:	mockingbird
STATE FLOWER:	bluebonnet

The Lone Star State

Word Scrambles

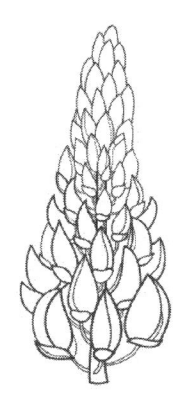

NUSTIN _____

DMIGOKINBRC _____

SUOTNOH _____

NEEBNTOBUL _____

GRNOOLHN _____

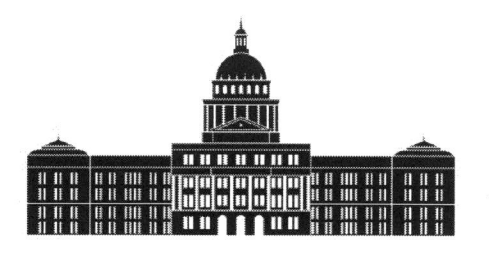

Word Match

Spanish — cattle

independent — State

Tay- — settlers

Lone Star — yas

12 million — nation

1. Spanish .... promoting Christianity, called missionaries, were some of the first Europeans to live in what is now Texas.

2. Texas became an independent .... called the Republic of Texas in 1836.

3. Caddo tribe greeted Spanish settlers by saying Tay-..............., which means "friends"—and sounds like "Texas."

4. Texas is nicknamed the .... State because in 1836, when the Republic of Texas declared itself an independent nation, it flew a flag with a single star on it.

5. Texas has about 12 million ...., more than any other state in the country.

Utah

Facts

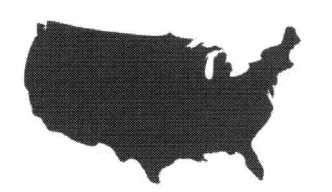

STATEHOOD: 1896; 45th state
POPULATION: 3,051,217
CAPITAL: Salt Lake City
BIGGEST CITY: Salt Lake City
STATE MAMMAL: Rocky Mountain elk
STATE BIRD: California gull
STATE FLOWER: sego lily

The Beehive State

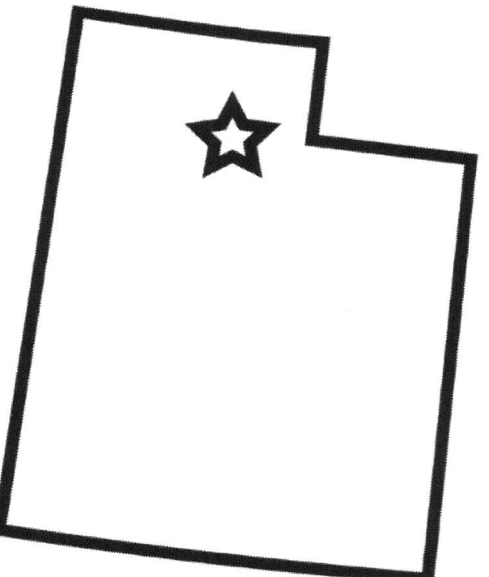

Word Scrambles

EOSG YLLIL   ____ ____

LUGL   ____

EBEEHVI EATST   _____ _____

HTUA   ____

KEL   ___

Word Match

people   Lake City

Salt   of the mount

Four   Corners

Beehive   State

sego   lily

1. Others say the name could come from the Ute word yutas, which is said to mean "the people," or "………………… of the mountains."
2. ………………… Lake City is the capital and most populous city of the U.S. state of Utah, as well as the seat of Salt Lake County, the most populous county in Utah.
3. Its southeastern corner touches Arizona, New Mexico, and Colorado. Called "………………… Corners," it's the only place in the country where four states come together!
4. Utah is nicknamed the ………………… State because the early pioneers considered themselves as hardworking as bees.
5. The ………………… lily is the state flower. Its bulbs were used as food by early settlers.

Vermont

Facts

STATEHOOD:	1791; 14th state
POPULATION:	624,594
CAPITAL:	Montpelier
BIGGEST CITY:	Burlington
STATE ANIMAL:	Morgan horse
STATE BIRD:	hermit thrush
STATE FLOWER:	red clover

The Green Mountain State

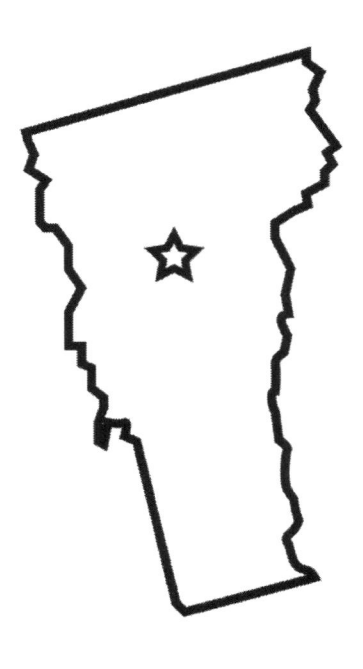

Word Scrambles

ELRVCO _ _ _ _ _ _

NMAORG _ _ _ _ _ _

URHSTH _ _ _ _ _ _

URGLNNOIBT _ _ _ _ _ _ _ _ _ _

ENOMERPTLI _ _ _ _ _ _ _ _ _ _

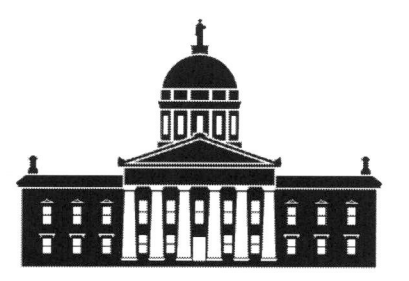

Word Match

Samuel — tree

French — Mountain Boys

Green — words

Mount — de Champlain

state — Mansfield

1. In 1609 French explorer .... de Champlain claimed part of the region for France.
2. Vermont's name comes from two .... words: vert, which means "green," and mont, which means "mountain."
3. The nickname honors the .... Mountain Boys, an army first created to protect Vermont's land from New York.
4. In the center of the state, the most famous range is the Green Mountains. Formed over 400 million years ago, the rocks are thought to be some of the oldest in the world. This range includes the state's highest point, ... Mansfield.
5. Vermont's famous maple syrup is made from sap from the sugar maple, the state ....

Virginia

Facts

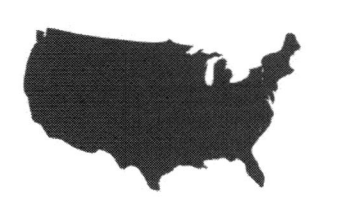

STATEHOOD:	1788; 10th state
POPULATION:	8,382,993
CAPITAL:	Richmond
BIGGEST CITY:	Virginia Beach
STATE DOG:	American foxhound
STATE BIRD:	northern cardinal
STATE FLOWER:	American dogwood

The Old Dominion State

Word Scrambles

DOL IOIONMDN   _ _ _ _ _ _ _ _ _ _ _ _ _

OHDRMNIC   _ _ _ _ _ _ _ _

CHABE   _ _ _ _ _

RNTHERNO   _ _ _ _ _ _ _ _

OGODDOW   _ _ _ _ _ _ _

Word Match

Thomas   Elizabeth I

Queen   Jefferson

Shenandoah   National Park

Mount   Rogers

American   dogwood

1. In 1776 famous Virginian, ... Jefferson, wrote the Declaration of Independence. And in 1788, following the Revolutionary War, Virginia became the tenth U.S. state.
2. Virginia was named after .... Elizabeth I, who was called the Virgin Queen.
3. .... National Park is a land bursting with cascading waterfalls, spectacular vistas, fields of wildflowers, and quiet wooded hollows.
4. Virginia's highest peak, is .... Rogers.
5. The .... dogwood is not only Virginia's official state flower, it's also Virginia's official state tree.

Washington

Facts

STATEHOOD: 1889; 42nd state
POPULATION: 7,656,200
CAPITAL: Olympia
BIGGEST CITY: Seattle
ENDEMIC MAMMAL: Olympic marmot
STATE BIRD: goldfinch
STATE FLOWER: coast rhododendron

The Evergreen State

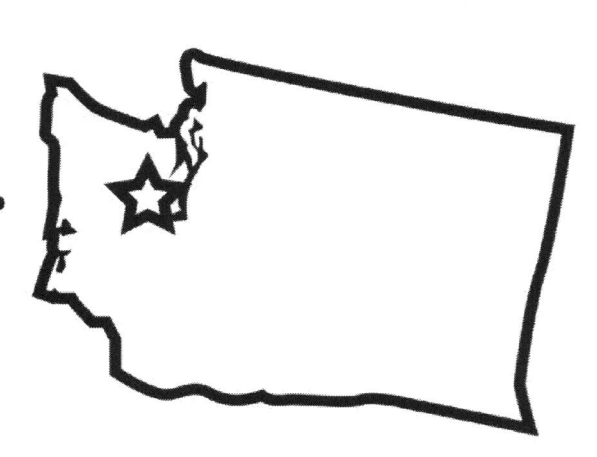

Word Scrambles

REEENRVEG   _ _ _ _ _ _ _ _ _
LFDGICONH   _ _ _ _ _ _ _ _
TEAETLS   _ _ _ _ _ _ _
YPAMILO   _ _ _ _ _ _ _
NONDERRDOHDO _ _ _ _ _ _ _ _ _ _ _

Word Match

George   State

Evergreen   National Park

Olympic   Washington

Coast   Range

Cascade   Mountains

1. Washington is named in honor of President .... Washington.
2. It's nicknamed the .... State because of its many forests, which cover over half the state.
3. The Olympic .... are located in Washington's northwest corner, which is bordered on the north by the Juan de Fuca Strait and on the west by the Pacific Ocean.
4. In Washington's southwest corner, the Coast .... area encompasses forested hills and beaches along the coast.
5. The Cascade .... , which include Mt. Rainier, are located further east.

West Virginia

Facts

STATEHOOD: 1863; 35th state
POPULATION: 1,831,102
CAPITAL: Charleston
BIGGEST CITY: Charleston
STATE MAMMAL: American black bear
STATE BIRD: cardinal
STATE FLOWER: rhododendron

The Mountain State

Word Scrambles

DEONDOHRNDRO   _ _ _ _ _ _ _ _ _ _ _ _

AACLNIDR   _ _ _ _ _ _ _ _

LETHOASNRC   _ _ _ _ _ _ _ _ _ _

ALBKC RAEB   _ _ _ _ _ _ _ _ _ _

NAGIRIVI   _ _ _ _ _ _ _ _

Word Match

West — gaps

Mountain — Virginia

water — J. Boreman

native — State

Arthur — wildflowers

1. West .... was originally going to be called "Kanawha," a name that honors a Native American tribe.
2. West Virginia is called the Mountain .... because it's the only state completely within the Appalachian Mountain region, and its average elevation is higher than any other state east of the Mississippi River.
3. West Virginia is known for its parallel ridges that were cut by streams, as well as canyons called "water ...."
4. The state has a large number of native ....
5. Arthur J. .... was an American lawyer, politician, first governor of West Virginia, and circuit judge.

Wisconsin

Facts

STATEHOOD:	1848; 30th state
POPULATION:	5,778,708
CAPITAL:	Madison
BIGGEST CITY:	Milwaukee
STATE ANIMAL:	badger
STATE BIRD:	American robin
STATE FLOWER:	wood violet

The Badger State

Word Scrambles

GBERDA ـ _ _ _ _ _ _
BONRI _ _ _ _ _
ETVIOL _ _ _ _ _ _
EWKIMEUAL _ _ _ _ _ _ _ _ _
SNIDOMA _ _ _ _ _ _ _

Word Match

meaning	roughly
15,000	Dewey
Timms	Hill
Nelson	Smith
Henry	lakes

1. Wisconsin's name might have come from a Native American word meskonsing, meaning .... "it lies red," or "this stream meanders through something red."
2. Wisconsin has more than 15,000 ....
3. Wisconsin's highest point is Timms ....
4. Nelson ...., 1813-1889, he was an American politician and the first governor of Wisconsin.
5. .... Smith, 1838-1916, he was a millwright, architect, builder, politician and United States house of representative from Wisconsin.

Wyoming

Facts

STATEHOOD:	1890; 44th state
POPULATION:	585,501
CAPITAL:	Cheyenne
BIGGEST CITY:	Cheyenne
STATE MAMMAL:	buffalo
STATE BIRD:	meadowlark
STATE FLOWER:	Indian paintbrush

The Equality State

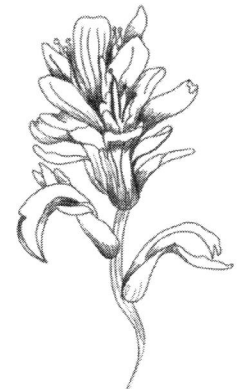

Word Scrambles

ECNHNEYE _ _ _ _ _ _ _ _

HSRPUANBIT _ _ _ _ _ _ _ _ _ _

LEOWKMDRAA _ _ _ _ _ _ _ _ _ _

ITEYQUAL _ _ _ _ _ _ _ _

FAULOBF _ _ _ _ _ _ _

Word Match

Devils Tower   paintbrush

Yellowstone   National Park

Red   of Wyoming

Indian   National Monument

Seal of the territory Desert

1. The Great Plains spread across the eastern part of the state and contains the Black Hills, where .... National Monument (the first national monument) stands.
2. The majority of .... National Park (96 percent) is located within Wyoming.
3. The Red .... is the largest living dune system in the United States.
4. Wyoming ....-paintbrush is a grayish-green, pubescent perennial with several leafy stems to 30 in. tall.
5. Seal of the territory ...., 1904, this seal has miners and horse riders in background, it also has two men on either side of statue, eagle and shield with strips. EQUAL RIGHTS is written on seal.

Notes

JUNIOR PRESS

ACTIVITY BOOKS FOR KIDS

We hope that our product has met your expectations. As a small family business, any review on Amazon would be very helpful for us. Thank you in advance.

Junior Press

Made in the USA
Columbia, SC
11 June 2025